It Gets Worse

ALSO BY SHANE DAWSON

I Hate Myselfie

It Gets Worse

a collection of essays by

SHANE DAWSON

Keywords
PRESS

ATRIA PAPERBACK

NEW YORK · LONDON · TORONTO · SYDNEY · NEW DELHI

ATRIA PAPERBACK
An Imprint of Simon & Schuster, Inc.
1230 Avenue of the Americas
New York, NY 10020

First Keywords Press/Atria Paperback edition July 2016

Keywords Press/**ATRIA** PAPERBACK and colophons are trademarks of Simon & Schuster, Inc.

For information about special discounts for bulk purchases, please contact Simon & Schuster Special Sales at 1-866-506-1949 or business@simonandschuster.com.

The Simon & Schuster Speakers Bureau can bring authors to your live event. For more information, or to book an event, contact the Simon & Schuster Speakers Bureau at 1-866-248-3049 or visit our website at www.simonspeakers.com.

Interior design by Dana Sloan

Manufactured in the United States of America

10 9 8 7 6 5 4 3 2 1

Library of Congress Cataloging-in-Publication Data

Names: Dawson, Shane, 1988- author.
Title: It gets worse : a collection of essays / Shane Dawson.
Description: First Keywords Press/Atria Paperback paperback edition. | New York : Keywords Press/Atria, 2016.
Identifiers: LCCN 2016002989 (print) | LCCN 2016016177 (ebook) | ISBN 9781501132841 (paperback) | ISBN 9781501132858 (eBook)
Subjects: LCSH: Dawson, Shane, 1988- | Comedians--United States--Biography. | Actors--United States--Biography. | Conduct of life--Humor. | BISAC: HUMOR / Form / Essays. | BIOGRAPHY & AUTOBIOGRAPHY / Entertainment & Performing Arts. | BIOGRAPHY & AUTOBIOGRAPHY / Personal Memoirs.
Classification: LCC PN2287.D39 A3 2016 (print) | LCC PN2287.D39 (ebook) | DDC 792.702/8092 [B] --dc23
LC record available at https://lccn.loc.gov/2016002989

ISBN 978-1-5011-3284-1
ISBN 978-1-5011-3285-8 (ebook)

For those who can't even.

Contents

About the Art

I have a lot of really talented fans. So I thought it would be fun to ask some of them to create pieces of art inspired by the essays. I sent each of them an excerpt and asked him or her to create whatever they felt like, using whatever medium they wanted. Throughout this book you will see a collection of drawings, paintings, balloon art, face painting, and even portraits made out of construction paper. Just like me, the art in this book is all over the place and sometimes shockingly weird. And I wouldn't want it any other way.

It Gets Worse

It Gets Worse: An Introduction

About the Artist

ALEXANDER T. GIESEN is a seventeen-year-old German-born British painter. His passion for art was first sparked in the eighth grade, after visiting a modern art exhibition. He currently is in his first year doing the International Baccalaureate diploma, where he studies fine art. The themes his paintings mainly illustrate are the problems that humans (especially women) in Western society face; this he shows by doing large-scale portraits with hidden metaphorical messages, often only conveyed through color or form. Follow him on Twitter @_alexrobins.

Hi, my name is Shane Dawson, and I'm here to tell you that it gets worse. It really does. The problems you have as a kid will seem ridiculous when you get older because bigger and worse problems will come along. But you will learn to deal with them easier as you grow up, or, like me, you'll just stop giving a shit. So yes, it gets worse, but you know what gets better? Your tolerance for bullshit.

When I was a kid I remember bad haircuts feeling like the end of the world. I would go into the salon with a picture of 'NSYNC and ask for the "Justin Timberlake." The stylist would look me up and down and then ask me what I thought about the "Joey Fatone." As an adult when I get a bad haircut, it doesn't even faze me. You know why? Because I'm just happy to have hair in the first place. Every man in my family was bald by age thirty, and I only have three more years to go. I have to enjoy this mane while I got it! I can only pray that in a few years I'll have enough hair to pull off a "Joey Fatone." Shit, at that point I would take a "Chris Kirkpatrick" and not bitch about it.

I also remember how big of a deal it was when someone at school bullied me or called me names. I was called fat, ugly, gay, momma's boy, albino, man tits, and once in a while rape baby. I don't quite understand that one, but then again, I kinda do. Little did I know then that nowadays the first thing that pops up when you Google my name is "Shane Dawson is dead." I mean, that's way past an insult. It means thousands of people have typed into their Google browser asking if I'm ALIVE. My young self probably couldn't have handled that, but at my age now, I really don't care. What's the point of getting mad about things when we are all just getting closer to death each day? Or, if you're like me, maybe you're already dead and you just don't know it yet!

In this book you will get to know even more about me than you did in my last book, *I Hate Myselfie*, mainly because I've learned so much more about myself since writing it. I've had my first real heartbreak that shook me to the core. I've directed my first movie and got panned by critics. One reviewer in particular called my movie "something only rapists, racists, and sociopaths could love." Ya, that was rough. But the biggest thing that has happened is that I discovered who I truly am and came out as bisexual. This past year has been a journey of self-discovery and also an attempt at self-love. If there's one thing I learned since my last book, it's that I don't hate myselfie. I just have moments of really being annoyed by him, and that's ok.

So sit back, grab a diet soda (Hey, we're all gonna die anyways, right?), and enjoy the stories that I'm about to tell to you. Just a warning, some of them might offend you and some of them might make you feel sick. But one thing is for sure, all of them will make you realize that even when it gets worse, there's still something to laugh about. And I find that pretty damn comforting.

—*Shane Dawson*

2 a.m.

About the Artist

STACIE GILBERT is a twenty-two-year-old animation major currently finishing up her degree online. Though she is an animation major, her passion is illustration and writing. She currently resides in the town of Lincolnton, North Carolina. You can follow her on Twitter and Instagram, both @Gilstacie, or you can find her at StacieGilbert.com.

I've always felt different from the other boys in my family. My oldest brother, Jacob, had a different girlfriend every month when we were growing up, and my other brother, Jerid, had posters of supermodels all over his walls. The only poster of a girl I had in my room was of Queen Latifah, and that's because I wanted to BE HER. She was so powerful. So tough. Like a bull. I wasn't the manliest boy, and I definitely stood out in family portraits. My brothers would wear baseball hats and have scraped knees from wrestling in the backyard, and I would have on a tie-dyed shirt with a fanny pack and early-onset arthritis from braiding my mother's hair every day. I was very skilled when it came to a French braid. They used to call me Red Lobster because the fishtails I was serving were ON POINT.

I remember my brother Jerid sitting me down when I was five years old and asking me a question that would be repeated throughout my childhood and into adulthood.

JERID: Shane, can I ask you something?
ME: Is this about the pee in your closet? Because I don't know who did that.

I peed in my family members' closets in the middle of the night till I was thirteen. It's actually kind of disturbing, and I should probably look into that. I'm sure I'm a sociopath.

JERID: No . . . Are you . . . gay?

Gay. I didn't even know what that meant. The only time I had heard that word was on TV when someone was using it as an insult. I didn't know what it meant, but I knew I didn't want to be it.

ME: No!

I ran to my room and locked the door. I curled up into my pillow and tried to forget about what had just happened. Luckily before long I heard the two words that could make me forget about anything unpleasant.

MOM: Pizza's here!

When I was in kindergarten I had my first crush, or should I say, first crushes. I walked into school with my hair slicked back and a Ninja Turtles lunch pail that was metal and super heavy. My mom wanted me to have a heavy lunch pail so I could protect myself with it. Even she knew I was a bully's wet dream. With my big, dorky glasses and my forty-year-old bank teller man hair I was just asking to get the shit beaten out of me. I walked into class, and I took a look around. My eyes stopped on what was the most beautiful girl I had ever seen in my five years of living. She had long blond hair and eyes that were so blue they looked like mirrors facing the sky. Her skin was soft and pale, and her outfit was perfectly color coordinated to keep her from looking even paler. Wait . . . maybe I am gay? Oh well. I walked up to her and tried to introduce myself, but before I could a boy with spiked, gelled hair and a douchebag face swooped in to steal my thunder.

It was at that moment that my world got more confusing. The boy looked up at me and said, "Go away, fat ass," and instead of crying, I just stared at him, completely awestruck. All the feelings I had for the girl I started having for the boy. Now that I think about it, there's probably some darker issue going on there considering he verbally abused me, but that's beside the point. I sat down at an open desk and started to panic. I had two crushes: one on a boy and one on a girl. And I could tell no one.

Instead of talking about my feelings to my family or my friends, I just bottled them up inside and pretended like they didn't exist. This became a common theme.

One night when I was around eleven years old, my brother Jerid and his friends decided to throw a party while my mom was working late. I was a goody-goody and was seconds away from calling my mom and ratting him out until they decided to order Chinese food and I would have sold my fat soul for some orange chicken. I had no moral code. After we ate pounds of greasy GMO-filled cat meat, my brother's creepy friend whipped out a VHS tape and everyone started freaking out with excitement.

CREEPY FRIEND: Guess what we're gonna watch?!
ME: *Flubber*?!

Silence. Wrong answer. I should have been aborted.

CREEPY FRIEND: No. A porno! I stole it from my dad's closet!

I was so jealous. The only things I ever stole from my dad's closet were shirts, since we both wore XXL.

My brother's creepy friend put the tape in the VCR, and it started to play. I don't remember much about the story line, but I do remember that there was a party and for some reason there was only one guy and twelve girls, which to me didn't seem weird because all my birthday parties were just me and a bunch of girls. Ya, my life was just like a porno. Except less sex and more "girl talk." The guy started to take off his clothes, and then the girls followed. All my brother's friends started laughing and shouting at the screen, and I just sat there in silence. I was trying to understand what I was supposed to be looking at. I wanted to look at the girls, but I also wanted to look at the guy. I was turned on by everything, and I was terrified by that. It was like I was at a Taco Bell drive-thru and everything on the menu looked delicious. I just wanted one of everything, with extra sauce.

A couple of years later, when I was thirteen, I had a conversation with my family that I'll never forget. I was getting ready to go into high school, and up until then I had never shown any interest in sex. I was always thinking about it, but on the outside I would never talk about my feelings. When anyone asked me who my celebrity crush was I would pick a person that was obviously a joke, like Oprah Winfrey or Rumer Willis. Sorry, Rumer. I was at a family get-together, and the topic of high school came up, and everyone turned their attention to me.

MOM: So, Shaney, you nervous about high school?
ME: I dunno.
UNCLE: They got showers there? If they do, I can teach you the family trick on how to make your penis look bigger.
ME: I'm good.

After a few more uncomfortable questions and a lot of terrible advice, a family member asked me the question that I had been avoiding since I was five years old.

FAMILY MEMBER: Shane, are you gay?

Silence. It was clear this was something they had all been talking about behind my back. Before I answered, I looked around and just about everyone in the room had a look of fear plastered on his or her face. My family was very religious, and being gay was seriously not ok.

ME: No.

Relief spread across the room. The only one who didn't appear relieved was my brother Jerid. He looked disappointed, like he knew I wasn't being honest with myself or my family. Later that night I went to the kitchen to eat some leftover Hamburger Helper casserole. There's nothing I love more than freezing cold Hamburger Helper at two a.m. God, I'm fucking disgusting. As I opened the refrigerator door I heard a voice behind me.

VOICE: Shane?

I jumped around and slammed the refrigerator door in shame.

ME: What?! I wasn't eating! I never eat! I just have fat genes!

Isn't that weird how you never see a fat kid eat? We always do it in private, as if we are fooling anyone. How sad. As my eyes started adjusting to the darkness of the kitchen I saw that it was Jerid.

JERID: Hey, man. Can we talk about something?
ME: Seriously, I have no idea who is peeing in your closet, but if you want, I'll help you look for them. It's most likely the same asshole who keeps eating the Hamburger Helper in the middle of the night. That sick fuck.
JERID: No, it's about what happened earlier today.

ME: When Aunt Carol asked if I was a C cup?

JERID: No, when someone asked if you were gay.

ME: Oh . . . that.

JERID: You know if you are, you can tell me, right?

ME: I know. It's just . . . it's confusing.

JERID: I love you, man. No matter what you like.

ME: I love you too.

I paused and started to tear up.

ME: I just don't want to go to hell.

I couldn't hold it in any longer. I started crying in the middle of the dark, cold kitchen. He grabbed me and held me while I let it all out. After a few minutes of my crying on his shoulder, he lifted my head up and looked at me with love in his eyes.

JERID: God loves you so much. Anyone that tells you different is an asshole.

I went back into his shoulder, and I felt so safe.

JERID: When you're ready, I'm here.

It would be years before I was ready to confront my feelings. I went through the next fourteen years holding them in and pretending that I was completely straight. I would fill the void in my heart with food and other addictions. Throughout my relationships with girls I would put walls up because I felt like I wasn't fully being myself. I had repressed my feelings for guys so far down that they started eating away at me. But as I grew up the world grew up. Fewer people were saying that gays were doomed to go to hell, and it was becoming more acceptable to be sexually open.

After my relationship with Lisa, my girlfriend of three years, ended I felt like I was ready to be honest with myself and confront the feelings that had been buried so deep. Our relationship hadn't ended because of my sexual confusion, but it hadn't helped either. I still believe she and I were meant to be in each other's lives as each other's rocks, but not in a romantic way. She's family to me, and she's one of the few people in my life I trust completely.

A few months after we broke up I asked her if we could talk about an issue I had been having, and she invited me over with open arms. I started to explain to her that I was feeling confused and that I wasn't sure how to define my sexuality. I broke down in tears and she held me and told me that she would support me no matter what. After that conversation, I started opening up about the topic with my therapist and even a few friends, but it wasn't until a late-night conversation I had with my brother that my life really changed.

It was two a.m., and Jerid and I were sitting in my apartment talking about life. We hadn't hung out in a few months, and we were just catching up on the latest.

ME: So what's goin' on?
JERID: Nothin'.
ME: Cool.

We always get super deep. After a few more minutes of small talk he got a little more personal.

JERID: So . . . what's going on with you, man?
ME: What do you mean?

JERID: You can talk to me about anything, you know that, right?

ME: Ya. Of course.

JERID: So . . . what's going on?

I knew where the conversation was going, and I was finally ready to be honest with him. We hadn't talked about my sexual confusion in fourteen years. Since that cold, dark night in my family's kitchen. I could feel my heart racing.

ME: I'm really confused.

JERID: I don't think you are.

ME: What do you mean?

JERID: You like guys, right?

ME: Ya. But I also like girls.

JERID: So you like both. Who cares?

ME: Well . . . I just wish I didn't. I wish I could just be straight. Or gay. It's so confusing to be in the middle.

JERID: Dude. You can't think of it that way. You're lucky. You can love anyone. Your options are doubled.

ME: Ya . . . I guess.

JERID: You ever been with a guy?

ME: No.

JERID: Go do it. Why the fuck not? You just need to be yourself and not give a fuck what other people think.

He made it sound so easy . . . and maybe it was?

JERID: Think about it this way, when you wake up tomorrow morning, how do you want to live your life? Hiding and ignoring your feelings like you have been forever? Or being yourself?

He was right. I smiled at him and he smiled back. It was the first time in a long time I didn't feel confused. I'm bisexual. All the years of thinking that it was a curse or that it was a phase I would grow out of were bullshit. There's nothing wrong with being open to love in any form. I felt a weight slide off my shoulders, and I started crying. But this time they weren't tears of pain or fear. They weren't tears of confusion or self-hatred. They were tears of happiness and the overwhelming feeling of being set free. From that day forward I wanted to live my truth, so I not only told my family and friends but I made a video about my journey to discovering my sexuality and shared it with the world.

This is me and there was no more hiding and there was no turning back. Thank God.

Best Buddies

About the Artist

ASHE YEBBA is a twenty-one-year-old self-proclaimed artist living in Omaha, Nebraska. Known on Tumblr for fandom art and specializing in ink mediums and anime styles, Ashe spends most of his time furthering his art skills by sketching as much as possible. Ashe has been following Shane since 2008 and jumped at the opportunity to share his art with Shane and fellow devoted fans. You can follow Ashe @AshleyYebba on Twitter.

Some people say high school is the most awkward and humiliating time of your life. Those people must have blocked out middle school, which marks the formative stage between childhood and adolescence, when you don't quite have acne but you definitely have prepubescent BO that smells like somebody threw up a Big Mac on a pile of pig shit. The smell that radiated off my twelve-year-old body caused my own mother to keep her distance from me. I remember one night when my mom sat on the other side of the couch while we watched *MTV Cribs*, which was very out of character for her because that was our favorite show to snuggle up to while we talked about our dream house.

Anyways, I knew that middle school was going to be a challenge for me. None of my friends from elementary school were going to be there because I had moved to another city after my parents got divorced. Most kids in my position would have been thinking more about the fact that their family had been torn apart and they were stuck between two fighting parents. I was more worried about having no friends to help me get my backpack out of the toilet after someone stole it and then peed on it. Which, by the way, actually happened to me. Except not only did someone pee on it, she perioded on it as well. I'm not sure if "perioded" is a word, but you get the point. It was graphic.

The night before my first day of sixth grade my brother Jerid sat me down to give me some very wise advice.

JERID: Don't wear black.

ME: Why?

JERID: You already have the face of someone who's gonna shoot up the school. Don't dress like one.

ME: Got it.

JERID: Also, don't use your pencil case. No one uses pencil cases.

ME: Then what am I gonna hold my pencils in??

JERID: Your backpack.

ME: Then what's gonna protect them from the pee and period blood?

JERID: What?

ME: My life is different than yours.

The next morning I woke up extra early so I could pick out something to wear that didn't make me look like a total idiot. FOUND IT! My SeaWorld shirt that had three dolphins swimming in a circle with the words "Poetry in Motion" on it. IN CURSIVE. Nailed it! While riding in my mom's car on the way to school I started thinking about all the things I was most nervous about, and I started sweating so hard that the dolphins were literally swimming in water. It was actually kind of beautiful, poetic if you will.

My biggest fear was the boys' locker room. The thought of changing in front of a group of guys made me want to jump out of my mom's car and get hit by a semi. Which, by the way, I used to think about every day. Thank God for child-safety locks. They're not just for curious toddlers, they're for sad, fat tweenagers with micro-dicks too. As my mom pulled up to my new prison she gave me a hug, while holding her breath to avoid smelling my tuna pits, and told me she was proud of me.

ME: For what?

MOM: For growing into such a wonderful man.

ME: But I'm only twelve.

MOM: Eh, you look thirty.

As I walked up the steps and into the gates I took a look around and noticed I was the only person wearing beautiful mammals on his shirt, and I felt pretty cool. Maybe this wouldn't be so hard. Maybe I would have a great yea—

DOUCHE: Nice shirt, dumb ass!

Ok, he didn't like it, but maybe someone els—

HOT GIRL: Poetry in Motion?! Here's a poem for you: Roses are red, violets are blue, I would rather choke on a coat hanger and die than fuck you.

I mean, I have to hand it to her. It was kinda good. As I walked to my first class I searched the halls, trying to find a familiar face. I knew my friends from elementary wouldn't be here, but maybe a kid I knew from my social life would. Of course by social life I mean the ball pit at McDonald's and the waiting room at my children's therapist's office. Unfortunately I didn't see any other fatties or crazies, so it was just me surviving this day alone.

A few hours later the lunch bell rang, and I had no idea what to do. If I were to sit in the grass patch by the quad alone, everyone would know what a loser I was. Although my shirt wasn't helping that situation. So I decided the only thing for me to do was hang out in the hallway and pretend like I was working on something. I'd rather people think I was an overachiever than a friendless mammal activist. So I took out my lunch and grabbed a notebook out of my backpack and started writing down nonsense. As I was on my third page of pointless scribble I heard a voice from behind me. It was a teacher, and her name tag read "Mrs. Rose." She was an older woman wearing a HIDEOUS cat sweater and an even more hideous wig. She looked like a crazy person you would see on a sitcom. You know, the lady who lives next door with eighty cats who plays marching band music out of her xylophone.

MRS. ROSE: That's a beautiful shirt.

I'm burning this shirt.

MRS. ROSE: What's your name?
ME: Shane.
MRS. ROSE: That's the name of my ex-husband.
ME: Oh. Cool. What was he like?
MRS. ROSE: He was a hero. He was eaten by rats while hiding from the enemy in a hole for two months.
ME: Wow, he was in the army?
MRS. ROSE: Nope.

Suddenly I wasn't the saddest person in the hallway.

MRS. ROSE: Are you in need of some company?
ME: Um . . .

There's nothing creepier to me than a student who hangs out with the teachers. I had one teacher in high school who would hang out with all the cheerleaders during lunch and buy them Quiznos on Fridays.

ME: I'm ok. Just working on my homework.

MRS. ROSE: That paper just has stick figures killing themselves on it.

Wow. I didn't even realize that's what I was scribbling. That's telling.

MRS. ROSE: Come into my classroom. There will be lots of friends for you to make.

She either had a room full of kids or a brain full of different personalities, but it was still better than sitting on a school floor with gum stuck to my ass. I got up and went into her classroom, and to my surprise there were real live kids! Although, I'm guessing she had multiple personalities too. That wig was definitely hiding some demons.

MRS. ROSE: Everyone, this is Shane. Let's all say hi to Shane!

The kids shouted my name in what I can only describe as a clusterfuck of noise and screams. I turned around and saw the sign next to the door, and it all made sense. This was a special ed class, and she thought I belonged here. I looked down at my suicide scribble for some ideas of how to fucking kill myself on the spot. Unfortunately there were no sharp objects to be found, and nobody was wearing belts because elastic shorts were all the rage in this room.

MRS. ROSE: There's a table back by the reading corner with an empty seat. Why don't you go on back there and meet some of the children? They don't bite. Well, Andre does, but only when provoked. He also tends to punch people in the genitals, but that's only when it's cold out.

I walked to the back table, and what I saw surprised me. There was a girl with long brown hair and beautiful blue eyes sitting reading a book. And it was a high school book, not a Dr. Seuss book with lots of pictures. My heart stopped and she put down the book and looked up at me. I was waiting in anticipation to see what was going to come out of her mouth. Were her words going to be slurred? At this point I didn't care. She was so hot I would have let her bite me in the face and punch me in the dick.

GIRL: Hi, my name is Cary.

My whole being went numb. She had the most beautiful voice, and her smile made me feel instantly safe. Something that I didn't feel too often as a kid. This was my moment to woo her. To let her know that I was her man and I was ready for the relationship to blossom.

ME: I'm not retarded!
CARY: What?
ME: I know. I mean, this shirt is retarded, but I'm not retarded. And I know I'm super fat, but I'm not like "retardedly fat," you know? I'm like . . . normal fat.
CARY: You should probably stop talking.
ME: Not that there's anything wrong with being retarded! I have retarded people in my family! I mean, now that I think about it, I probably got some retarded genes passed down to me. I definitely have been told I have a retarded person's forehead.
CARY: Can I talk to you in the hallway real quick?

I could tell I had messed up. Her face was red and it was squinched in anger in a way that reminded me of the times my mom discovered I'd tried on her lingerie while she was at work. I was in BIG TROUBLE . . . and also had therapy again on Monday.

Cary dragged me into the hallway and closed the door tightly behind her so none of the students could hear.

CARY: What the fuck is wrong with you??

ME: Do you want a list or . . .

CARY: Do you know how offensive the word "retarded" is?

ME: A lot?

CARY: Ya, a lot! And you said it like thirteen times. And what the hell do you mean by a retarded person's forehead?

I lifted my hair up.

CARY: Oh . . . Ya, I guess I can see that.

ME: I'm sorry! I was just nervous! I really do know . . . mentally challenged people, and I would never want to hurt their feelings. I just couldn't shut up, and you're so . . . so . . .

CARY: If you say "retarded," I'm gonna pull an Andre and punch you in the tits.

ME: I thought he punched in the crotch?

CARY: Oh, maybe that's something he only does to me, then.

ME: I don't blame him. I'd punch you in the tits all day if I could.

She looked creeped out. Probably should have just said "retarded" again.

ME: I'm sorry. Can we start over? I have no friends, and I really don't want to spend the rest of the year eating on the floor and having people throw food on me 'cause they think I'm a trash can.

CARY: That happened?

ME: No, but it will. Some people say that when they see me from the
   corner of their eye, I look like trash.

CARY: Wow, that's dark.

ME: Ya, my grandma gets kinda mean when she misses a pill. One
   time she told me from far away I looked like the bus.

CARY: Ok, then. Well, let's start over. Hi, I'm Cary.

ME: Hi, I'm Shane.

CARY: Nice to meet you.

She smiled. I smiled back. We had a moment. It was nice. Next
step, she would be my girlfriend and I would love her forever.

ME: Can I ask you a question? You seem really cool, and pretty, and
   normal. Why are you hanging out with the special ed kids?

CARY: Well, my brother is mentally handicapped and I wanted to do
   something in school to help out people that were struggling like
   him. So I decided to join the Best Buddies program.

ME: What's that?

She walked me back inside the classroom and explained the program, which was really amazing. It was a club where students would
come in during lunch and spend time with the special ed kids. And
it wasn't an educational thing. They didn't read to them, or teach
them math, they just hung out with them. Treated them like peers.
Just chilled with each other and didn't act like anyone was different. Because, as Cary put it, "we're all the same and we're all just
as fucked-up as each other." A statement I couldn't have related to
more.

After hanging out with her for that lunch period, I decided that I
wanted to join the club. Mainly because it sounded like a really cool
way to give back, but also I wanted to see Cary get punched in the tit

by her buddy so I could jerk off to it later. This was before Internet porn existed, so don't judge me.

The next day during lunch I walked into Mrs. Rose's class and spotted Cary sitting in the back reading her book. I walked up to her, but before I could get her attention Mrs. Rose stopped me in my tracks.

MRS. ROSE: Shane! I'm so happy you decided to join Best Buddies!
ME: Thanks! I'm gonna go hang out with Cary and her buddy!
MRS. ROSE: Um, Shane. You don't need to hang out with Cary's buddy! You get your own buddy!

For some reason that thought hadn't crossed my mind. I figured I would be hanging out with everyone. Being in charge of one person terrified me. The one time I'd ever babysat, the kid ran into a glass door and got a concussion. And I laughed. I wasn't made for this.

ME: Maybe I could just be like . . . everybody's buddy?
MRS. ROSE: That sounds exactly like something my ex-husband used to say. And do I need to remind you what happened to him?

Rats. Hole. Dead. Moving on.

ME: Where's my buddy?!

She turned around and grabbed a student from a desk. As the student stood up I noticed the name tag on his desk. Andre. The dick-punching, face-biting, eight-foot-tall guy whose dick I could see through his elastic shorts, and it was HUGE. It looked like a toddler hiding behind window curtains. I started to panic. I was not cut out for this. I'm sure he was a sweet kid, but he could literally EAT

ME. He was the tallest person I had ever seen. His head was the size of a train and his teeth looked like the passengers.

MRS. ROSE: Andre, say hi to Shane!
ANDRE: Hi.

BOOM! His voice was so low it ricocheted against the walls and made all the desks vibrate. It was like that scene in *Jurassic Park* where the *T. rex* roars in the face of those kids and they all shit themselves. There was a serious chance I had shit myself too.

ME: Hi, Andre. Nice to meet you.
MRS. ROSE: Put your hand out, Shane.
ME: WHAT?
MRS. ROSE: Put your hand out so Andre can shake it.

PUT MY HAND OUT? Are you fucking crazy?? I'm sure he's sweet, but if he grips my hand with his, it will look like the Jaws of Life CRUSHING a Kia Soul! And I can't lose my right hand! That's the hand I do all my . . . scribbling with.

CARY: Come on, Shane. Shake his hand.

Cary was now standing next to me with a smile on her face. She was loving this. The look of sheer terror plastered across mine was giving her pure oxygen. She was living for it.

ME: Ok. Let's do this.

I put my hand out to shake his, and . . . he shook back. It was fine. He didn't crush me. He didn't punch me. He just shook my hand, smiled, and let me go. I felt like a total piece of shit. I couldn't believe for a second I had been too scared to treat him like a human being. Just because he was an actual giant and had the voice of a ship horn didn't mean—

ANDRE: BALLS!

CRUNCH! He jabbed my junk and started crying laughing. Cary started to bust up and even Mrs. Rose couldn't hold her laughter. Finally, Cary reached over and placed her hand on my shoulder.

CARY: Welcome to the club, Shane.

Over the next month I went to the classroom every day during lunch and we had the best time with each other. Andre was actually super hilarious and really cool to talk to. He had such an interesting life. His family had moved six times in one year and I related to that a lot. Since my parents divorced I had moved a few times and it was really hard on me. I couldn't imagine dealing with that on top of needing special attention. He was a really extraordinary guy, except for the occasional violence. One day we received an assignment from Mrs. Rose.

MRS. ROSE: Ok, everyone, I thought it would be fun if this weekend you took your buddy out for a fun time! Maybe a movie, or a lunch date, or even a ball game at the park! What do you think?

Everyone was super excited about it. Especially Andre. He gave me a hug and squeezed me tighter than I had ever been squeezed before. It was similar to the footage you see on Animal Planet of the anaconda SUFFOCATING the goat and swallowing him whole. It was definitely a sweet and terrifying moment that made my sad life flash before my eyes.

I didn't really have anyone to hang out with on the weekends, so I was also excited about this task. Maybe Cary and I could have a double date with our buddies? There was only one way to find out.

ME: Hey, Cary, what are you and your buddy gonna do this weekend?
CARY: We're gonna have a sleepover at my place. You know, girl stuff. What about you?

Crap. She's busy and I had nothing planned.

ME: Same.
CARY: You're gonna have a sleepover with Andre?

Didn't think that one through.

ME: No! We're gonna do guy stuff. You know . . . play with Beanie Babies and probably whip something up in the Easy-Bake Oven.

I didn't know much about guy stuff.

CARY: Cool. Well, have fun, freak.

The bell rang, and it was time to go back to class. She smiled at me as she left, and I couldn't stop smiling back. I needed to ask her out soon, but I didn't know how. What if she just saw me as a . . . buddy?

That night I was having my man date with Andre. My mom and I drove over to pick him up and he ran out of his house in a way that reminded me of another scene from *Jurassic Park*. You know, the one where the *T. rex* runs toward the truck and then eats everyone inside?

MOM: That's your friend?
ME: Yep! Big, huh?
MOM: It looks like a toddler hiding behind window curtains.

He got in the car, and my mom took us to the movies. I'm about 90 percent sure my mom thought we were on a date, and I was ok with that. I mean, Andre was a catch, and let's be honest, I was lucky to get what I could get.

As Andre and I waited in the theater for the movie to start we started engaging in "man talk."

ME: Do you think Cary likes me? You know, likes me likes me?

Sorry, spelling error. I meant "girl talk."

ANDRE: Ya. She likes everyone! She's so nice.
ME: Ya . . . but I mean . . . you know . . . LIKES me.
ANDRE: Like the way I like Mrs. Rose?
ME: I hope not.
ANDRE: Have you asked her?
ME: No way! What if she says no! What if she laughs at me! What if she makes you punch me in the dick?
ANDRE: You should ask her to the fall dance. I'm gonna ask Mrs. Rose.
ME: Fall dance? That's a thing? Also, you really gotta find a new crush. You know, something not illegal.
ANDRE: The fall dance is coming. It's my favorite dance 'cause there's candy corn everywhere.

ME: Now you're speaking my language. I fucking love candy corn.

ANDRE: Also Mrs. Rose always saves me a slow dance.

ME: You're creeping the fuck out of me, Andre.

That Monday Mrs. Rose told us what our next assignment would be. We were in charge of being our buddies' guardians at the fall dance. This was perfect! It was the perfect time for me to ask Cary if she wanted to take our relationship to the next level.

ME: Hey, Cary, will you go to the dance with me?

CARY: Oh . . . you mean like . . . as a . . . friend?

ME: Um . . . Um . . .

I started to sweat, and I heard a grunt behind me. It was Andre shooting me a "you got this" face. I turned back around to meet my destiny.

ME: No. As more.

CARY: Oh.

OH?! What do you mean OH?! She used the same tone I would have if I found out it was past eleven a.m. and McDonald's wasn't doing breakfast anymore!

CARY: I just don't want to date right now.

ME: Oh.

My "oh" was more in the tone of just hearing that MCDON-ALD'S HAD JUST BLOWN UP AND THEY WERE NEVER COMING BACK!

CARY: I'm sorry. I just don't want to date until I'm fifteen. We're still
    kids, you know.
ME: But I look thirty.
CARY: I'm sorry, Shane.

She gave me a hug. Not as tight as an Andre hug but just as
sweet.

CARY: Still friends?
ME: Hey, best buddies.

We laughed, but on the inside I was dying. It was the first time
I had ever had the courage to ask a girl out, and I got shot down.
Luckily Andre was there to lift me up.

ANDRE: Mrs. Rose said yes!
ME: What?
ANDRE: Told you she liked me.

Once again my mentally handicapped friend's life was better
than mine. The next week was the dance and I made sure to find the
coolest outfit I could. Unfortunately I'd thrown my dolphin shirt in
a fire pit and watched it burn to fucking ash, so all I had left was the
outfit I'd worn to fifth-grade graduation. It was a button-up shirt and
pants that had a rip in the ass. Still a step up from the dolphin shirt.
    My mom dropped me off at the dance, and I saw Andre standing
at the door waiting for me. He looked awesome. He had on a suit
and the shiniest shoes I had ever seen. He looked like a member of
OutKast, and I looked like a guy from *American Idol* who lived in his
car and got voted out the first week. As we walked in together, lots

of girls were hitting on Andre and staring at his . . . toddler. I tried to make the sexiest face I could, and all I got was a teacher asking me if I was ok. She even mentioned that the nurse was on duty. Once again, nailing it.

CARY: Hey, Shane! Hey, Andre!
ME: Hey! Where's your buddy?
CARY: She's on the dance floor. I can't get her off.
ME: Isn't she . . . deaf?
CARY: Ya! She feels the vibrations of the beat through her feet!

I looked over at Cary's buddy and she looked like she was in an old-school Britney video. Her arms were popping, her hips were shaking, her head was whipping. She was a true pop icon reincarnated. Of course the deaf girl was a better dancer than me, and my buddy had a bigger dick than me. Special ed kids: 2. Me: 0.

CARY: Are you gonna dance?
ME: Nah, probably not. Just gonna make sure all the buddies are safe. Maybe have some punch or something.
CARY: Well, I'm going to dance, so if you wanna join, that's where I'll be.

I wanted to be there more than anything. Dancing with her. Watching her hair fly through the air as she jumped around to the beat. It sounded like heaven. Too bad I was a big pussy who watched everyone else have fun while I ate deviled eggs by the trash can. You know, eating the innards and throwing away the white. A big pop song came on and busted through the speakers. I don't remember the song, but I do remember it was something everyone knew and everyone wanted to dance to. I saw all the best buddies RUSH to the dance floor and take over. I was nervous because I didn't want the other students to make fun of them. Kids can be so mean. Hell, just a couple of months ago I might have even laughed at a group of special ed kids freak-dancing on each other. But after spending time with them and becoming their friend I just wanted to see them have fun and be happy. And that's what they were doing. Mrs. Rose's whole class was in the middle of the dance floor fully having the time of their lives. Not caring what anyone was thinking about them. Not listening to the laughter coming from some of the "normal" kids, and not even paying attention to anyone around them.

As I watched I felt inspired. I wanted to be more like them. I wanted to not care what other people thought. I wanted to just be myself and ignore all the assholes that surrounded me. I decided to throw away my last deviled egg and make my way to the dance floor. I saw Cary, and she was jumping up and down like she was in the middle of a rave. She looked so free and so happy. I ran up to her and started jumping too. She screamed over the music.

CARY: YOU'RE DANCING!
ME: YA, I KNOW!
CARY: YOU SMELL LIKE EGGS!

I shut my mouth to keep the smell from coming out and kept dancing. She laughed and then grabbed my hands. We started jumping up and down and spinning in circles. Besides the fact that deviled-egg-colored vomit was starting to come up, it was the most fun I had had in a long time. I felt like I'd found my place.

For the rest of the year I spent each day hanging out with Cary and the rest of the buddies and I never had to eat lunch alone again. I also started wearing a crotch cup on cold days just in case Andre experienced a fit of rage. Luckily I had a micro-dick, so not much damage could have been done anyways. I'm not sure where Andre is now, but I'm sure his life is better than mine in every way. That good-looking, tall, hung asshole.

• • •

Special ed kids: WINNERS. Me: 0.

The Lottery

About the Artist

STEPHANIE SHAW is an eighteen-year-old fine arts student, originally from Liverpool, now studying in London and hoping to go on to study effects makeup and prosthetics. She's had a paintbrush in her hand for eighteen years and has slowly moved from painting on paper, to canvas, to . . . well . . . her own face. Lover of horror and gore as well as musical theater and costume design, she's completely honored to have her work chosen and published. She can be found on her Instagram @stephanie.shaw.art.

It was a typical Sunday morning. While most eleven-year-olds were watching cartoons I was watching the Spanish channel because the coat hanger I had shoved in the back of my television didn't feel like picking up Nickelodeon that day. The telenovela dramatically unfolding featured a couple screaming at each other in their living room while their three daughters watched with tears in their eyes. A lamp was thrown across the room and smashed through a window. The father slapped the mother in the face but not before the mother stabbed him in the stomach with a carving knife. While all of this was happening, the family's television set was showing a music video on MTV. As the father took his last dying breath in front of his screaming children, I had only one thought: Does that family know how lucky they are to have CABLE?? They can watch *whatever* they want *whenever* they want! It's like they're living the dream! I'd watch my mom brutally kill my dad if it meant I could watch cartoons in HD.

When my family and I wanted to watch something on TV, we had to play a game of eeny, meeny, miny, mo to see who would risk getting electrocuted by shoving their fingers in the outlet to steal cable from the neighbors. Sometimes it worked, but usually it ended with one of us needing an ice bath and a two-day nap. Cable was one of the many luxuries that we couldn't afford in my house.

By the time I was eleven, I was living with just my mom and my brother Jerid. We had a nice routine set for Super Cheap Sundays.

We would go to church so we could get all our lessons from the Bible and soak up the beautiful word of Christ. Just kidding. We went to church because they had free donuts and hot chocolate. The word of Christ was just something you had to sit through so you could get your glaze on. After that we would return home and go to our separate areas of the house. My mom would do laundry, my brother would go back to sleep, and I would stare out my bedroom window and try to watch the couple who lived in the apartment across from us having Sunday-morning sex. As it was the day of the Lord, they would usually steer clear of anything too experimental.

But this particular Sunday morning was different. Instead of spending my day trying to catch a glimpse of Veronica's asshole (I'm not sure if that was her name, but it's nice to give a name to the people you spy on. It makes them more real.), I was interrupted by my mom, who burst into my room with an enormous smile on her face and a Bible in her hand. It was as if she had discovered the meaning of life, and I was the first person she was going to tell.

MOM: Shaney! We're going to win the lottery!!!

Fuck the meaning of life! This was even better! This bitch discovered MONEY!

ME: What?!!!
MOM: Jesus told me in a dream!
ME: That sounds literally insane, but I don't care! I want to see what a hundred-dollar bill looks like!
MOM: I prayed to him last night, and when I went to sleep I had this incredible dream that we were going to win the lottery and be able to do everything we've ever wanted. It was so real. I think it was a sign.

ME: Wow. Do you think you can ask Jesus to make me skinny?

MOM: He's not a miracle worker, honey. Now go get on some clothes! We're going to the liquor store!

It was at that moment I realized I could put all common sense on the back burner if someone dangled money in front of my face. Even as a kid, I should have known how impossible the odds of winning the lottery are, but I didn't care. All I could think about was how I was going to buy that douchebag kid in my class from his parents (everything has a price) and make him spend the rest of his life getting his hairs slowly picked out of his head by my fat little fingers. Of course I'd have to set some money aside for the creepy-ass basement I was going to need to keep him in. Oh, and obviously some money set aside for my college. I was reasonable.

As we hopped in the car my mom's eyes were full of hope. I hadn't seen that look in years. The last few years had been difficult after my dad left, and her eyes were usually too tired from working her nine-to-five job to show any signs of spirit. Seeing her like this was refreshing, even if the circumstance was a little crazy. As we drove to the liquor store we started talking about which six numbers we would choose for our ticket.

ME: Did Jesus tell you what the winning numbers were?

MOM: No. Maybe we just choose random ones and pray they're good?

ME: That's how I feel when I pick a dish out of Grandma's cupboard. I pray to God she washed at least one of them in the last twenty-five years.

MOM: Maybe we should pick our birthdays?

ME: Good idea! Let's do mine, yours, Grandma's, Jerid's, and Jacob's! Twelve, twenty-three, nineteen, twenty-nine, eight.

MOM: Perfect!

ME: Wait, we need one more!

MOM: How about seven. That number's special.

ME: 'Cause that's how many times we saw *Titanic* in theaters together?

MOM: No.

ME: Because that's how many Weight Watchers points my favorite donut at Krispy Kreme is?

MOM: No.

ME: Because that's the age I was when strangers finally stopped thinking I was a girl?

MOM: Awwww, you'll always be my husky little girl.

She pinched my cheek. I pinched my inner leg, which is like cutting for people who don't like blood. Try it.

MOM: Seven is the number of completion in the Bible. It's how long it took Him to create the world. Maybe us winning the lottery will be the completion of our struggles. We can start over again. Start a new life.

I looked at her with admiration. She was so convinced that this was going to happen, and I was really starting to believe it. I've never believed in anything as much as she believed that God was going to perform a miracle to get us out of our debt. It was like watching a kid on Christmas wait for Santa Claus to crawl down the chimney. As we pulled up to the liquor store she did the sign of the cross over her forehead and reached over and did it over mine. This is still something I do to this day. Every time I get on the freeway I do the sign of the cross over my forehead, and it always makes me feel safe. Even though I'm not as religious as I once was, I still feel connected to God and I still want His protection. It's like using a toilet-seat cover at a nice restaurant. You know deep down that nobody who can afford to eat there has ringworm, but you don't want to risk it.

When we pulled into the liquor store parking lot, we could see a line of people wrapped around the building. My mom stopped the car near a woman who looked just as desperate for cash as us.

MOM: Hi, is this the line for lottery tickets?

DESPERATE WOMAN: No shit. What did you think this was? A line for pretzel dogs?

ME: Honestly, I wouldn't be surprised. The new fiesta blast flavor is kind of revolutionary. And just a tip: try dipping it in the cheese from the nacho station. It's fifty cents extra, but it really enhances the experience.

DESPERATE WOMAN: Wow, the employees here have gotten so much more helpful!

ME: I'm eleven.

We parked the car and walked to the back of the line to wait our turn. I noticed the line was full of all types of people, similar to what you might find at a Christmas parade. Everyone had hope in their eyes, but they all secretly knew it would be a letdown. Think about it: Have YOU ever been to a parade and left satisfied? Have you ever turned to your friend and said, "Wow, that wasn't a total waste of fucking time"? No, you have not. No one has. Parades are the same as the "professional" beat boxers that go on TV talent shows. Loud, depressing, and useless.

When we finally made it up to the counter, the man handed us a ticket and asked us to fill out our numbers.

ME: We're gonna win today! God told us!

EMPLOYEE: Really? That's exactly what that guy said.

He pointed to a homeless man peeing in the parking lot, aiming his penis into his mouth. My expectations for winning started to slip. We wrote down our numbers and gave the ticket a good-luck kiss, and my mom tucked it into her Bible. We got back into the car and headed home. The winning numbers would be announced in eight hours, and I couldn't contain myself. On the drive back to our apartment all I could think about was what I would spend the money on if we won. Obviously, I would give some to charity, possibly give that homeless man who talks to God a bottle to pee into. But after that, what would I do? Maybe a new bike? Or maybe an Easy-Bake Oven? I was always too scared to play with one, but with that much money, who cares how many people made fun of me! I could just BUY acceptance from my peers! I looked out the car window as we drove past a nice neighborhood, where I saw an OPEN HOUSE sign.

ME: Mom. We should go to that open house!
MOM: Oh, Shaney, we could never afford that. This is the fancy neighborhood.
ME: Umm . . . Mom.

I pulled the lottery ticket out of her Bible and waved it around. She smiled and flipped a U-turn. It was time to start spending our invisible money! As we passed a street full of mansions I couldn't help but wonder what life was like on the other side. What was it like to wake up in the morning and open a fridge full of brand-name foods and then sit on your couch that was from a store and not from the curb while you watch cable that you had gotten LEGALLY? This was a world I had no experience in, but I was ready.

We pulled over in front of a house with balloons and a sign in front of it. As we walked up the driveway I looked up to take it all in. It was the biggest house I had ever seen in my life, and I suddenly wasn't sure I was ready for it. Even though we believed we were going to be rich in the next eight hours, we were still technically poor street trash. What if the real estate agent saw us walking through the door and then kicked us out for smelling like coupons?

ME: Maybe we shouldn't go in.
MOM: Why not? This is our dream house!
ME: What if they make fun of us? What if they know we're poor?
MOM: If we want to fit in, then we have to act the part. Stand up straight.

I pushed my shoulders back and pumped up my chest.

MOM: Push your hair back.

I spit in my hand and used it as a gel to slick my hair back.

MOM: Now make a face like you just smelled your own fart and liked it.

That one was easy for me. Farts are like little gifts from your body. It's the same way I feel about pimples or pickable foot skin. Hours of free entertainment.

MOM: Alright. Now let's go in there and be stuck-up assholes like the rest of them!

When we walked inside, the first thing we saw was a sign-in sheet and a gold pen sitting on top of it. I grabbed it and scribbled down our full names. "Boobies McTitface" and "Mrs. Queefington." Give me a break, I was eleven. As we turned to take our tour of the house a woman wearing a pantsuit and a stick up her ass stopped us for a chat.

MRS. PANTSUIT: And you are?

ME: McTitface. And this is Mrs. Queefington.

My mom looked at me, pissed. She obviously hadn't read the sign-in sheet, but it was too late. The queef had already been released.

MOM: Yep, that's us. Just a couple of successful business people.

ME: I invented marshmallow Peeps.

MRS. PANTSUIT: Aren't you ten?

ME: Eleven, actually. But thank you. My VERY expensive face cream must be working.

MRS. PANTSUIT: Right. Well, if you have any questions, please let me know.

As the woman walked away, my mom and I busted out in laughter. We had officially lost our minds, but at least we were having fun. This was way better than waiting for Veronica to finish Jason off with a handy. (Once again, not sure if that was his name, but he looked like a Jason.)

We walked into the living room and gasped as if we had seen heaven with our own eyes. The room was bigger than our entire apartment. Hell, it was bigger than our whole building! The TV was the size of a movie screen, and the couch looked big enough to do belly flops on. The walls were covered in art that wasn't bought at the "House and other stuff" section at Goodwill. It was everything we had ever dreamed of, and it was all ours. Except it wasn't, and we were literally in someone else's house. But who cares, we were just dreaming. I jumped on the couch, and my mom took a seat in a reclining chair.

ME: Mom! This couch doesn't smell like gasoline!

MOM: And this chair reclines without going all the way back and throwing me out of it!

At that moment we both did the sign of the cross. This is what we wanted more than anything, and we believed in all our hearts it could happen. As we left the house we got in the car and started talking about the pros and cons as if we were really considering buying it.

ME: Ok, pro, it had a big living room.
MOM: Con, the bedrooms were leaving a little something to be desired.
ME: I agree. The master didn't even have a walk-in shower.
MOM: I mean, if I'm gonna have a master shower, I need at least four shower heads.
ME: Totally, and how am I supposed to fall asleep with that loud fountain gurgling outside my window? I think our backyard should have a waterslide and a realistic rock-climbing mountain, not a loud, outdated fountain. Who are we, the mob?
MOM: Agreed. Not our house. But we'll find something better.

It's funny how fast money can change you, even when it's invisible.

ME: You know what I just realized? We can't pull into our new driveway in an old shitty car.
MOM: You're right! We need to upgrade.

On that note we decided the next reasonable car to bring into our family was a brand-new 1999 Hummer. You know, one of the biggest, most expensive cars a person could own in the nineties.

They also completely destroy the environment, but hey, we were rich! We didn't care about the earth! We could buy a spaceship and live on the moon!

We pulled into the Hummer dealership and parked our sad, half-dead Saturn in the parking lot. We got out and dashed away from it as if it was about to explode. Mr. McTitface and Mrs. Queefington wouldn't be caught DEAD in that trash can on wheels! As we walked around the dealership and looked at some of the biggest cars I had ever seen, my mom turned to me and made a confession.

MOM: These are pretty cool. But you know what I really want?

ME: A husband?

MOM: Well yes, but also a Chevy SUV.

ME: Really? But those aren't fancy. Those are just normal cars.

MOM: I guess I'm not really a fancy lady.

ME: Ya, me neither. That last house had a water fountain in the bathroom. I mean, the water was cold and it was nice to rehydrate after taking a pee, but it was a little much.

MOM: That was an ass cleaner.

ME: That makes more sense.

We left the Hummer dealership without test-driving anything. Sure, we wanted to be rich, but we weren't interested in becoming the Hiltons. It was Sunday, so it was going to be a family dinner, which meant my grandmother was on her way over. My mom usually cooked something, but since tonight was going to be a special night, we decided we were going to go out to eat instead. It was our last night as members of the lower class, and we had to celebrate it in true lower-class style. HomeTown Buffet! Me, Mom, Grandma, and my brother Jerid sat around an E. coli–covered booth and talked about what our futures had in store for us, other than food poisoning.

GRANDMA: So you really think you're going to win the lottery?

MOM: I really do.

GRANDMA: That's the stupidest thing I've ever heard, and I watch *The View*. The other day one of the women said that dogs can read, and THIS is stupider than that.

ME: Grandma, just have faith!

GRANDMA: The only thing I have faith in is that when I go over there to refill my soup bowl, they'll have fished out that goddamn cockroach from the chowder pot. And I'm not even so sure about that.

My brother Jerid chimed in.

JERID: You really think we're gonna win, Mom?

MOM: I do. I feel like God was telling me that our life is going to change, and we are going to get so many amazing gifts.

JERID: Can I get a skateboard?

MOM: Of course! We can get a whole skateboard park!

JERID: Really?! What about a ramp in my room?

MOM: That sounds incredibly dangerous, but why not!

JERID: I might break my neck, but who cares! I can buy a new one!

GRANDMA: Wait, you can buy a new neck?

JERID: You can buy anything if you're rich.

GRANDMA: What about new legs?

JERID: Anything.

The expression on my grandma's face turned from doubtful to hopeful. Even though she still felt deep down this was ludicrous, the thought of being able to walk without crutches gave her so much excitement that she put her doubt on hold for the night. Over that meal we talked about everything we were going to buy with our fortunes, and we even told the waitress that we would mail her a thousand-dollar tip. I'm pretty sure she thought we were insane and most likely hallucinating from the amount of chemicals in our overprocessed food, but it didn't matter. Our heads were up in the clouds, and nothing could bring them back down to reality.

When we got home, it was 6:55 p.m. and we were five minutes from finding out the winning numbers. We all gathered around the TV and continued to talk about our new rich life that we were about to enter. And then the conversation took an unexpected turn.

JERID: So how much should we give to the rest of the family?

ME: What do you mean?

JERID: Like aunts and uncles and stuff?

GRANDMA: Fuck 'em! They aren't here!

MOM: Mom! Don't say that!

GRANDMA: What? They didn't buy the ticket.

MOM: Well, neither did you.

GRANDMA: So what? Are you saying you aren't going to give me any of the money?

MOM: Not if you keep saying selfish things like that.

ME: Guys, please! It's almost on. Let's just pray.

JERID: What about our friends? Can I give my friend Mike some money? He shares a bike with his little sister, and honestly, it's embarrassing. It has streamers on it and a bell.

ME: My bike has streamers and a bell.

JERID: And do I ever ride with you?

ME: No.

GRANDMA: Well, I think I should get a new house because I gave my old house to you!

MOM: You didn't give it to me, we bought it from you!

GRANDMA: And then you lost it!

MOM: Don't bring my bankruptcy into this!

ME: Guys, the numbers are being announced!

Everyone was heated and upset, but we all directed our attention at the TV. My mom kneeled on the floor and started praying as hard as she could. My grandma was still mad, so she had her arms crossed, ready for a fight. I held my breath as the woman on TV slowly took numbered balls out of a rotating container.

WOMAN ON TV: The first number is . . .

You could hear everyone's hearts beating in our living room. Our lives were about to change in a matter of seconds.

WOMAN ON TV: Twenty-four!

Or not. Jerid looked down at our ticket.

JERID: We don't have twenty-four.

My mom didn't even hear him. She was so focused on her prayer that the only thing she heard was the sound of her own voice asking God for a miracle. As the woman on TV continued reading numbers that weren't ours my heart slowly began to break. With each number a dream disappeared.

WOMAN ON TV: Three!

There goes our dream house.

WOMAN ON TV: Fifteen! .

and my king-size bed.

WOMAN ON TV: Six!

my Easy-Bake Oven.

WOMAN ON TV: Two!

my ranch-dressing fountain.

WOMAN ON TV: Seventeen!

and my mom's dream car. A Chevy SUV.

They were all gone. My mom came out of her trance and turned to us all sitting on the couch.

MOM: Did we win?

My brother walked out of the room and went back to bed. I started to cry as I stared at the ticket, willing the winning numbers into existence.

GRANDMA: Of course not. That was ridiculous. What a waste of time.

My grandma headed to the bathroom. I could tell she was disappointed, but she would hide her real emotions with anger. For a split second I think she believed that we were going to win, but she had let her greed get the better of her. We all had. My mom crawled over to the couch and sat next to me. Tears were streaming down her face. She looked broken.

MOM: You must think I'm an idiot.

I didn't know what to say, so I just put my arms around her and let her cry on my shoulder. I didn't think my mom was an idiot. I thought she was desperate. Desperate for a miracle to come and help her family. Desperate for God to answer a prayer and give her new hope. Desperate for somebody out there to hear her prayers and come save us. I didn't think that dream my mom had was bullshit; I just think she interpreted it wrong. Our life was going to change, just not yet. That night I learned a lot about money and what it can do to people. Even though we didn't have it in our hands, we were already letting our greed take over and tear our little family apart. That night taught me so much and made me realize how I wanted to handle money if I was ever blessed with it. I wouldn't spend it like an idiot and let it ruin my relationships. It's not worth it, because when all the money in the world is gone, all we are left with is ourselves, and I really didn't like who we had become that night.

Ten years later my mom's dream came true. After working hard on YouTube, I started to have financial success, and I was able to do something for her that I had never thought possible. By that time, I had already taken care of my family by moving us to Hollywood and getting us a nice place to live, stocking our refrigerator with brand-name foods, and most importantly, getting us cable. But there was one thing I had been wanting to do for years that I was finally able to.

One Sunday night, I walked into my mom's room with an enormous smile on my face, similar to the one my mom had that day ten years prior.

ME: Mom! I have something crazy to show you!

MOM: Oh no. Please don't pull out another dildo. I just did my daily Bible study.

I liked to buy my mom dildos and film her reactions. We had fun.

ME: Seriously! Come look!

My mom followed me to the front door with a suspicious look on her face.

MOM: What are you doing? Is this for a video? Should I do my hair? I look like cra—

Before she could finish her sentence I opened the front door and revealed a brand-new Chevy SUV sitting in front of our house. She looked at me, confused. I took the keys out of my pocket and placed them in her hand. Before I could say a word, her eyes filled with tears and she grabbed me for a hug.

ME: I know you've always wanted one.
MOM: You got me my dream car??
ME: It's all yours.

The feeling I got from buying my mom the car she had always wanted was the best in the world. But it felt so good because I had worked so hard to get it. If we had won the lottery that day, we wouldn't have appreciated the millions of dollars thrust upon us. Every morning when I wake up in a nice bed with a nice breakfast to eat, I know that I can't take it for granted and I need to appreciate what I have. I know what it's like to have nothing, and I know what it's like to wish for a better life. At the age of twenty-one, I was able to change my family's life for the better, and we didn't need the lottery to do it. I don't think God played a prank on my mom that day when He told her that she was going to win the lottery. I think He just didn't tell her when it was going to happen. She never lost faith that one day we were going to have everything we ever wanted, and she was right. Her dream came true. Now if she could just have a dream that six inches was considered *super well-endowed* then I'd really be set.

Chub Rub

About the Artist

BRIANA MARINO is currently a freshman in college. She became interested in art around her sophomore year of high school, and that's how she decided to become a graphic design major. Shane inspired her to be the creative person she is today.

chub rub— When the skin between a fat chick's thighs rubs together while walking, causing a mild irritation between her legs.

Used in a sentence: *Yo, I thought that chicken head had some cooties but it was some mad chub rub.*

—*Urban Dictionary*

I t was a warm September evening in 2006, and I was lying in bed with my pants off and the door locked. The steam coming off my sweaty, fat body had fogged up the windows and turned my bedroom into a hotel resort sauna. Except instead of fancy wood-paneled walls covered in Asian-inspired artwork, picture, if you will, asbestos-filled walls covered in termites and Hilary Duff movie posters. *Titanic* was on, and it had just gotten to the scene when they have hot, intense sex in the back of a car. As Rose's sweaty hand SLAPPED the fog-covered window my sweaty hand SLAPPED my naked thighs and covered them in rash cream.

If you are assuming my eighteen-year-old self was having a sexy night alone, you are wrong. It was the night before my first day of college, and I was medicating a serious case of chub rub I had gotten earlier that day. I had been walking through Macy's—ok, Al's Big and Tall—trying to find an outfit. After hours of hunting for the perfect body tent, I developed a rash. It's something every overweight person is familiar with, and it's one of the most annoying things that can happen during the summer. Well, that and having to keep coming up with new interesting excuses for why you don't want to go to the beach. No shoes, no shirt, no Shane.

The fact that I was going to college was a shock to me because I had never thought about it as a kid. Every time a teacher in middle school would say, "Ok, kids, this is to prepare you for college," I would ignore them and daydream about how I wanted to die. My ideal death was decapitation by a machete. Is that normal for a kid to think about? Probably not. But is it any more bizarre than a twelve-year-old thinking about going to college? You shouldn't be thinking about college when you're in sixth grade. You should be thinking about not getting the shit beat out of you by the kids who call you "walking mayonnaise."

My parents never pressured me about school. Hell, they never even talked to me about it. I'm pretty sure it's because they didn't go and no one ever sold them on the benefits of an education. I remember one time when I was thirteen, I asked my mom if I should go to college, and it turned into a very confusing conversation.

ME: Mom, I was thinking about where I should go after high school.
MOM: Are you trying to tell me you want to move out?
ME: No, I—
MOM: 'Cause I need you here! If you're not here, then who am I gonna have date night with? And who's gonna eat the rest of the Hamburger Helper when I make it?? It makes SIX servings, Shane! And there's only ONE of me!

I'm sure from reading my first book you already know how unhealthily close my mom and I were, so I'm just going to keep moving. Near the end of high school I decided to apply to college because all of my friends were doing it. I wasn't too passionate about the idea, but I figured I would give it a shot. I picked a school close to my house because I knew I couldn't afford to move away, and let's be honest, the Hamburger Helper wasn't gonna eat itself. I was told by a guidance counselor that I should apply to more than one school, but my mom could only afford to help me apply to one, so we put all our eggs in that basket. As I was about to click send on my online application my mom kneeled down next to my computer desk and grabbed my hand to pray.

MOM: God, please have Shane be accepted into this college and let him succeed and follow all of his dreams.
ME: Amen.
MOM: Also, let me find a man. Preferably one who's not an alcoholic or a chain-smoker. And let him just pop into my life. Maybe a pizza man? Or a bag checker? I would even settle for a war veteran with PTSD who thought I was trying to kill him.
ME: Amen.

After a few weeks of waiting I finally got a letter in the mail from the college, and I ran into my apartment so I could open it with my mom. We were both shaking, and before I even finished reading the first sentence we started ugly crying. HARD.

ME: Dear Shane, we are pleased to inform you—
MOM: AHHHHH! THANK YOU, JESUS!

Our cries were so ugly you would have thought we were two cripples who'd just had an Extreme Home Makeover.

A few months later I had a talk with my guidance counselor about what classes I was going to take my first year of college. That's when I found out I had to take three years of general education before I could apply for the film department, and there was still a chance after that that I wouldn't get in. And if that happened the whole three years would have been for nothing. I didn't have a plan B. Being a director was all I ever wanted. I had a gut feeling that college wasn't for me, but I decided to put those thoughts on the back burner and focus on the fact that I got into college in the first place.

A year later I was in my room, covered in rash cream, watching Jack and Rose make love while I thought about my first day of school. I was pretty terrified because I had no idea what to expect. The only things I knew about it were what I had learned from movies. I knew that I was gonna gain "the freshman fifteen," which to me was nothing. Fifteen pounds? I could gain that on a Friday night at the Souplantation if I played my cards right. The next thing I knew was that someone was definitely going to try to sell me drugs. Although I'd been told I had the face of a forty-five-year-old police-woman, so most kids thought I was a narc. The last thing I knew was that there was going to be a lot of walking because the campus was so large and spread out. That's what I was most nervous about. I got a rash walking around a department store; how would I survive a college campus?

Instead of freaking out, I decided to focus on what I was excited about . . . which was nothing, so I went to bed and covered my rash in an adult diaper.

The next morning I woke up with a smile on my face, mainly because I'd had a dream about being decapitated by a machete. As I drove into the college parking lot, I looked at the other cars and they were just as shitty as mine. I felt like maybe I would fit in just fine. I got out of my beat-up ride and looked at the campus map to see where I was going first. I put my finger on the parking lot and then dragged it all the way to the orientation office. I started doing the math in my head, and the mathematical conclusion I came to was . . . DAMN, THAT SHIT'S FAR. I took a deep breath and began my journey.

As I walked through campus I took in all the sights around me. I saw hot guys making out with hot girls. I saw ugly guys making out with ugly girls. I even saw an ugly guy making out with a semi-decent girl. There was hope for me! Sure, she had a back brace and what appeared to be face ringworm, but she had a pretty decent body. I took a little break on a bench after walking for what felt like hours and looked down at the map. I was only halfway there! I felt like I was walking around Disneyland, but it was more expensive and the only ride was a roller coaster of emotions you get when you find out the suicide rate! My chub rub had started to flare back up, and it wasn't helping that I was wearing jeans. I should have known not to wear denim, but I was so concerned about looking cool that I ignored my instincts.

I've had a long history with denim and chub rub. It all started when I was ten years old. My mom was dating a guy who was always trying to impress us. I remember one time when we were all together for a day out he pulled his car over to an ATM, hopped out, and said, "I love spending money!" In my opinion, he was a keeper. I have no idea how great his relationship was with my mom, but this motherfucker had a heavy-ass wallet and I wanted to help him go bankrupt. One day when we were all eating at a restaurant he looked over at me and asked a question I'll never forget.

MONEY GUY: Hey, Shane, tell me something crazy you want to do today?
ME: Steal you away from my mom and have you buy me an island.

Obviously I didn't actually say that out loud, but I definitely thought it. Can you imagine me having my own island? Shirts would be mandatory, and the volcanos would be filled with cheese dip.

ME: Um . . . ride a roller coaster?
MONEY GUY: Let's do it!

He drove us down to Knott's Berry Farm and we embarked on a day filled with roller coasters and no lines. He bought us the front-of-the-line VIP passes because he REALLY wanted to fuck my mom. And I wanted him to. I could only imagine what kind of amazing things he'd buy me if he was tapping that. We decided to go on a water ride, and that's when the day took a turn for the worst. I was wearing my jeans and I had a little chub rub already, but the second my jeans got wet all hell broke loose. Wet denim makes a rash ten times worse. I'm sure there's been some scientific study about it. Most likely funded by the Khaki Committee. I don't care how fat I get, I'm not wearing khakis. That's the epitome of giving up on life.

As we left the water ride and headed over to get funnel cakes I couldn't hold my pain back any longer. My thighs were burning so badly I broke down and started crying. I fell to the floor with tears streaming down my face and started grabbing at my rash-covered legs.

MOM: Shane, what's wrong?
MONEY GUY: Is it something I said? Was it the comment about you kind of looking like a cartoon bear at certain angles?
ME: What?
MOM: I don't think he heard that.
ME: No, it's . . . it's . . .
MOM: Honey, tell us.

As I pointed down to my legs my mom knew exactly what it was and she knew how embarrassed I was by it. What kid wants his future sugar daddy to know that his fat legs had rubbed together so hard they literally started a flesh fire?

MOM: I think we should go home now. It's been a long day.

MONEY GUY: But . . . I wanna spend more money.

As much as I wanted to drain his bank account and make him buy me a pony, I was in too much pain to have any more fun. My mom took me home and helped me put on my rash cream. And I'll never forget her advice that night as her hands were lathering up my inner thighs.

MOM: No jeans when it's hot out.

Now, as I sat on the college bench feeling the familiar burn between my legs, I knew I should have listened to her advice. I was starting to feel defeated. It was only the first day and I was already in pain from walking around campus. I started having doubts about going to college. I could barely afford the application fee; how was I going to afford everything else that came along with it? Especially since I could tell I was going to need A LOT more chub rub cream than usual.

Just as I began to spiral down a dark hole of self-pity, a security guard walked up to me and struck up a conversation. He was around fifty years old and looked like this was definitely his second job, his other job being a rapist.

SECURITY GUARD: Hey. I haven't seen you around here before. This your first day?

ME: Ya. I'm a freshman.

SECURITY GUARD: Freshman?! I thought you were a security guard!

Told you. Narc.

ME: Ya, I get that a lot. Especially at malls. It's one of the reasons I'm too scared to ride a Segway. I don't want to constantly be stopped and asked where the bathroom is.

SECURITY GUARD: Ya, security is hard. What you studying?

ME: Film. Well, not yet but hopefully soon. I have to take general education first.

SECURITY GUARD: Cool. You gonna make really sad movies?

ME: No, why?

SECURITY GUARD: Just figured.

ME: Ok . . . Well, I'm gonna go to class now.

SECURITY GUARD: Let me walk you!

ME: Oh, I'm ok.

SECURITY GUARD: It's more for your safety. You're just asking for an ass whooping wearing that shirt.

Did I mention I was wearing a shirt that said "SLICE to meet ya!" with a smiling cartoon piece of pizza on it? I wish I could kick my own ass. As we walked toward my class the chub rub started to get worse. I could literally feel pieces of my skin falling off. It was like two sticks rubbing together starting a campfire, and my "s'more" was starting to smell like fish.

ME: Is there a bathroom around here?

He looked at me for a moment, confused.

ME: Men's.

Confusion over.

SECURITY GUARD: Oh ya! Right over here.

I walked into the bathroom and checked under every stall to make sure I was alone. All clear. I turned on the faucet and started to unbutton my pants. The rash had gotten so bad it felt like steam was coming from my jeans when I lowered them down. My thighs looked like they had a third-degree burn! For some reason I thought covering them in cold water would make them feel better, but I should have learned from my ten-year-old mistake: WATER AND DENIM MAKE IT WORSE.

As I washed my rash with the cool water I felt a little relief, which was instantly ruined once I pulled my pants back up. It felt like I had just put on a pair of pants made out of knives and grandpa face. You know, that thick rough grandpa skin that you feel when he gives you a drunken kiss on Christmas? No? Just me? Anyways. I walked out of the bathroom clutching my thighs like I had just been kicked in the nuts.

SECURITY GUARD: Did someone beat you up in there? Maybe turn that shirt inside out? I can't be with you 24/7.

ME: No. I'm having kind of a personal problem. Do you happen to know if there's a pharmacy on campus?

SECURITY GUARD: Of course, man. That's where they got a bowl of free condoms! Which really comes in handy when you're surrounded by this many fine-ass women.

ME: Aren't you fifty?

SECURITY GUARD: You're as young as you feel!

ME: I don't think that applies in this situation.

I walked into the pharmacy and searched everywhere for rash cream, but I couldn't find it. I was desperate, so I went up to the girl at the register to ask.

ME: Hi, I need rash cream.

GIRL: This is college; you're gonna have to be more specific.

ME: I'm not sure what the medical term is.

GIRL: There's nothing to be embarrassed about. I've heard it all.

ME: Chub Rub.

GIRL: Eww, what the fuck?

I'm pretty sure she thought I had some kind of STD only trans-mitted by fat people. Great.

GIRL: Follow me back to see the nurse.

I was so glad to know college was filled with so many open-minded, nonjudgmental people. What a nice change from high school. As we walked into the nurse's office I was instantly relieved by her warm, welcoming smile. She was like a school nurse out of a movie. She had suckers on her desk in case anyone got nervous as well as different-colored bandages to make wounds more fun.

NURSE: How can I help you?

ME: I'm having a situation and I need some rash cream.

NURSE: Is it an allergic reaction?

ME: No . . . it's more of a wearing-jeans-and-having-fat-legs reaction.

In that moment I could tell she understood me. She wasn't a thin woman herself, and she definitely wasn't wearing jeans.

NURSE: Gotcha. I've got just the stuff.

She reached into her medicine cabinet and grabbed a bottle of ointment that had clearly been used, most likely on her.

NURSE: This should do the trick.

ME: Thank you so much.

NURSE: So, how's your first day going?

I hesitated. It wasn't going well. I hadn't even made it to my first class and I was already in the nurse's office for a crotch burn.

ME: Not great.

NURSE: You wanna talk about it?

ME: I just . . . I don't know if college is my thing.

NURSE: What makes you say that?

ME: Well, first of all, the campus is huge. And I know this sounds crazy and incredibly lazy, but I'm not sure I can survive walking this much every day. I might actually die.

She laughed. I didn't. That much walking would have actually killed me. And "walking to death" wasn't even on my top-ten list of ways to die.

NURSE: What else is bothering you?

ME: It's just . . . I don't know if college was a good idea. I only applied because nobody in my family ever had. I wanted to prove to myself that I could get in. And now that I'm here, I'm not feeling good about it.

NURSE: What are you majoring in?

ME: That's the thing. I want to major in film, but it's going to take three years of general education before I can even apply for that.

NURSE: Oh, so you want to be a director?

ME: More than anything.

NURSE: Well, I'm sure you know how hard it is to get into that business.

ME: Ya, trust me. I know it's a long shot, but it's all I ever wanted.

NURSE: What about a plan B?

ME: Never. The day I think of a plan B is the day I've given up. Well, that and the day I start wearing khakis.

She laughed and sat down next to me.

NURSE: I want to tell you something. Not as a nurse, but as a friend.

ME: Ok.

NURSE: If you really want to be a director, you're not going to learn about it in a classroom.

ME: What do you mean?

NURSE: You have to experience it. Get on a movie set and learn how everything works in the real world.

ME: Wait . . . Are you telling me to drop out?

NURSE: I'm telling you to go with your gut. And if your gut is telling you to make movies, then that's what you have to go do. Not sit behind a desk for three years hoping that maybe you will be accepted into the film program.

I thought about what she was saying, and it really hit home. I didn't want to be in college. I was so proud that I had been accepted, but the idea of being trapped in a classroom terrified me.

ME: You give a lot of people this speech?

NURSE: If I did, I would have been fired a long time ago.

ME: Thanks.

NURSE: Don't mention it. Lollipop?

ME: Ya, fuck it. Why not?

She smiled and handed me a lollipop. I popped it in my mouth, took the bottle of cooling cream, and walked out the door. On the way back to my car, I called my mom to tell her about my decision. I was scared she would be disappointed in me and feel like she failed as a parent, but instead her reaction was exactly what I needed.

ME: Mom, I'm dropping out. I want to get a job and support myself while I make short films and learn filmmaking on my own.

I heard ugly crying on the other end. But they weren't sad tears; they were happy ones.

MOM: I'm so proud of you, Shane.
ME: Really?
MOM: I was praying about it because I knew your heart wasn't in this. You don't need college to tell you you're a director. You've been one since the day you held up a camera for the first time when you were ten years old.
ME: Thanks, Mom.
MOM: One day you're gonna make a movie like *Titanic* and inspire a kid to be a director just like you.

That night I went home and lay on my bed with my pants off and turned on the second half of *Titanic* while I covered my thighs in rash cream. As I watched the ship crash into the iceberg I knew that I had made the right decision. My goal wasn't to have a college degree or for a professor to tell me I had talent. It was for an audience to see my stuff and connect with it. I knew that if I just started working hard, I would get there, and I would learn along the way.

From that day forward I started posting monthly videos on You-Tube and learned everything I could have ever hoped to learn in college. I learned how to edit, produce, and write scripts, act, and even build an audience.

I'll always be grateful for chub rub. It caused me pain and embarrassment, but it truly changed my life and forced to me to take a huge risk. And without it, I wouldn't be here today.

Now this isn't meant to make anyone feel like college is a waste of time, because for so many people it's not. But don't go because you feel like you have to. If your heart isn't in it, then why spend four years of your life stuck somewhere you don't want to be? If you're passionate about something, give it your all, and you will find happiness. Whatever you do, just remember not to wear jeans if it's hot out. And wear anything but khakis. That's giving up before you even get started.

Friends Without Benefits

About the Artist

KYLE ZARBOCK is eighteen years old and has been interested in art since he was very young. Currently, art is his entire life. He is taking many art classes at his high school, including a college credit Advanced Placement art class. He is going to major in art in college, and hopes that one day his art will be a part of something bigger, whatever that may be. Hopefully, one day he can do what he loves for a living.

Social media with his art:

Facebook art page: kylezarbockart

Tumblr: youre-not-listening

Instagram: mouth_full_of_white_lies

By the time I was twenty-two years old, the only person I had ever been in love with was Andy the waitress at the Cheesecake Factory, and that was because she knew to bring me ranch along with my bread basket for dipping. She never judged me for it. Because that's what love is: no judgment. But besides her, I had never felt love for anyone besides family and friends. As a kid I had crushes, but I would never act on them. Mainly because I knew that there was no way in hell they would be interested in me. I mean, what kind of kid is interested in a guy whose grandma still wipes his butt at age twelve? I know that sounds disgusting, but trust me, she loved it. It gave her purpose.

In high school I didn't have many crushes, but the ones I did have were way out of my league. Well, any girl who didn't have a cleft palate or a back brace was out of my league. By the time I was a senior, I was still a virgin, as revealed during a game of Truth or Dare one Friday night.

We were sitting in a circle in my bedroom as Avril Lavigne was playing in the background. Her music really was the soundtrack to my childhood. I always felt like I was extremely *complicated* and I was just trying to live my *sk8er boi* life. Except in reality my life was sadly straightforward, and I had never ridden a skateboard, because I was scared I would break it. Everyone was laughing at our slutty friend Tara, who had just been dared to put a TV remote in her vagina and change a channel. Not only did she change a channel but she set my DVR to record *Teen Mom*. She was a true American hero. Then it was my turn, and all eyes were on me.

TARA: Ok, Shane, truth or dare?

ME: Um . . . I dunno. If I choose dare, will I have to get naked?

The whole room screamed, "EWWWWW," and "DEAR GOD!"

ME: A simple "no" would have been fine.

TARA: Come on, Shane, pick dare! Don't be a pussy!

ME: I'm not a pussy!

TARA: You have a five-CD changing stereo and all five CDs are Avril Lavigne.

ME: So!

TARA: She only has two albums.

ME: The others are B-sides and live performances . . . Ya, I guess I'm a pussy.

TARA: So? What do you say?

ME: Fine . . . dare.

The whole room clapped excitedly. I had never been a risk taker, so my friends were ready to see me do something crazy.

TARA: I dare you to go in the closet and make out with Sara for two minutes.

RANDOM FRIEND: Isn't it supposed to be seven minutes?

TARA: I love Sara too much to do that.

ME: Thanks.

TARA: So, what do you say, Shane?

ME: Um . . . I'm not sure. Can I do a truth?

TARA: Oh, come on! Stop being a pussy!

ME: I'm not a pussy!

TARA: Don't make me go through your CD collection!

She was right. I was a pussy. And not just because I had the deluxe edition of Lindsay Lohan's "Confessions of a Broken Heart" with two bonus tracks and a poster. It's because I had never kissed a girl, and I was terrified.

ME: Please. Just give me a truth. I'll answer anything—I promise!

TARA: Fine, truth. Why won't you kiss Sara? Is it 'cause you have a crush on her?

The whole room *oooooooooh*s like a bunch of toddlers.

ME: No. She's not even my type.

TARA: Who is your type?

Girls with blond hair. Guys with kind eyes but a mean streak. It's complicated. Avril complicated.

ME: I don't know.

TARA: So then why didn't you kiss her?

ME: Because I've never kissed before.

The room got quiet.

TARA: Really? Not even a relative?

ME: I mean, sometimes my uncle gets drunk and plays with my boobs, but he never slips me the tongue.

TARA: How have you not killed yourself yet?

ME: Food helps.

Later that night it was just Tara and me lying on the floor in my room talking about the party. Everyone had already left and we were recapping.

TARA: Can you believe Allan picked up a quarter with his asshole?

ME: And he sang the alphabet backward while doing it. He's so talented. It's not fair. All I can do is suck air into my butt and fart it back out. And I'm not even sure that's a talent. I think it might actually be a medical condition.

TARA: Speaking of weird things you do, were you serious about never being kissed?

ME: Ya. I know it's a shock. How could a guy with lips this chapped and bloody not have people sucking all over them?

TARA: Your lips *are* always bleeding. You should probably get that checked.

ME: I'll make sure to mention it to the doctor after he checks out my anus vacuum.

We both laughed, and then it got silent. Tara lifted her head up from the floor and rolled over onto my chest. She looked at me with love in her eyes like she was about to tell me she had feelings for me. I clearly remember my heart started to race, and my boobs started to sweat.

TARA: Shane. You know I love you, right?

ME: What?

TARA: You know, as a brother.

ME: Oh. Ya. Of course.

TARA: Because I love you, I want you to know that I would do anything for you.

ME: Like give me a kidney?

TARA: I was thinking more like a blow job.

Annnnnnd my boobs were puddles.

ME: What?!

TARA: I know you have never done anything like that, and I know you really want to. And I know you probably won't find anyone to do it for you until you grow up and get all rich and successful, so I thought I could help.

ME: I thought you were gonna offer to kiss me!

TARA: NO! That's way too special! You have to save that for someone you love.

ME: And sucking my dick isn't?

TARA: Please, sucking dick is nothing. Like a hand job or fingering. Literally meaningless.

ME: Wow. I want to live in your world.

TARA: So what do you say?

She put her hand on my zipper and started to move it down.

ME: Thanks, but because I love you like a sister, I think it might be kinda weird.

TARA: Ok, well if you ever change your mind, I'm here for you. Just think of me as your mouth to fuck.

ME: I'm sure many people do.

Five years later, the closest I had come to getting a blow job was sticking my dick in a pool drain and getting it stuck. At twenty-two years old I was ready to finally get intimate with someone, and unfortunately I hadn't kept in touch with Tara, so I had to go elsewhere. It was a Friday night and I was at a party full of YouTubers, and

I definitely wasn't looking for any potential relationships. This was also before being a YouTuber was "cool" and "glamorous," so the vibe of the party was a little less Kardashian and a little more *Duck Dynasty*. There wasn't a photo booth with cool props to post on your Instagram, and there sure as hell wasn't a Taco Bell truck with free burritos till three a.m. It was just twenty YouTubers, a bucket full of beer, and lots of people vlogging. It's what I imagined hell to be like, and all I wanted to do was leave.

As I was making my way out, I saw a girl standing on the porch waiting for her ride. As she turned her head I noticed her instantly. She was a YouTuber who I had been cyber-stalking for months. She had the softest-looking hair I had ever seen. It was like a horse jumping through the sky, which, by the way, you should never tell a girl, because it did not go over well.

ME: Wow. Your hair is so long. It's like a horse.
YOUTUBE GIRL: You're saying I look like a horse?
ME: No! Just your hair. But not in a bad way.
YOUTUBE GIRL: How is that not bad? Don't horses lie in their own shit?
ME: They also have penises the size of traffic cones!

Girls also don't like it when you compare them to something that has a monster dick.

ME: Let me start over. Hi, I'm Shane.
YOUTUBE GIRL: I know who you are! I'm just messing with you. I get your humor.
ME: Really? That's amazing! Most girls would have slapped me if I compared them to a farm animal.
YOUTUBE GIRL: Well, I grew up on a farm, so I consider it a compliment.
ME: You did? That's awesome!

I already knew. I had seen all her videos and knew her entire backstory. Number of siblings. Names of parents. Age of first period. I was a walking Wikipedia page for this girl.

YOUTUBE GIRL: We should hang out sometime. I just moved to LA, so I'm looking for friends.
ME: Of course! I'd love to. Just let me know when and I'll bring my saddle! Unless you wanna go bareback?

I laughed. She didn't. Too far.

YOUTUBE GIRL: Well, I'll see you around, cowboy.

As she rode off in her friend's car I couldn't help but notice her hair flying out of the window, looking like a horse galloping across the desert. It was beautiful, and all I wanted to do was ride her.

. . .

DING. The next day I got a text from my horse-haired goddess. I jumped out of bed and unlocked my phone. I was like a kid on Christmas, and I was hoping to finally get the pony I had always asked for.

TEXT FROM YOUTUBE GIRL: Hey Shane. Wanna hang out tonight?

I gasped in excitement. I ran over to my computer and started playing "I'm with You" by Avril Lavigne. Some things never change.

TEXT FROM ME: Sure! My barn or yours?
TEXT FROM YOUTUBE GIRL: Really? Still?
TEXT FROM ME: Sorry.

We decided to meet at her place and watch a movie. Up until this point I had never been on a date, so I had no idea what to expect. I wasn't even sure this was a date. I asked my brother for some advice.

ME: Do you think it's a date?

BROTHER: Is it just you and her?

ME: Ya.

BROTHER: Then hell ya. Why else would a guy and a girl hang out if it wasn't to try and fuck?

ME: To be friends?

BROTHER: That's what ugly people say.

ME: Oh.

BROTHER: Ugly people are friends. Pretty people fuck. Sometimes a pretty person fucks an ugly person, but that's usually for karma points or because they have daddy issues. Does she have daddy issues?

ME: I don't think so.

BROTHER: Hmmmm . . . then she must need some serious karma points.

As I drove up to her house I started to get nervous. I started thinking of all the ways I could mess this up, most of which included me showing her my butt vacuum. I tend to do it when I get nervous.

DING-DONG. I rang the doorbell, and after the longest ten seconds of my life she opened the door. She looked incredible, and I was speechless. The only sound my body made was the WHOOOSHING sound from my ass sucking up all that air.

YOUTUBE GIRL: Wanna come in?

WOOOOOOOOOOSH.

YOUTUBE GIRL: I'll take that as a yes.

We walked inside and sat on the couch. We talked for hours about life, being a YouTuber, and how hard it was to explain to people what we did for a living. I can't imagine being a hot girl and having to tell people that you make internet videos for a living. That has porn written all over it. The night felt really casual and it didn't feel like a date at all, and that's because it wasn't. She genuinely just wanted to hang out with me and make a new friend. I was disappointed but at the same time relieved because I would have had no idea what to do if she had made a move on me. I probably would have jumped on her back and kicked her in the ribs. I don't think that would have gone over too well.

For the following few months we hung out almost every night. We watched movies, baked cookies, and even went grocery shopping. It was almost like we were married, except we didn't have sex, so it was EXACTLY like we were married!

One night we were watching TV in her room and she rested her head on my shoulder. Uh-oh. I could feel the boob sweat coming back. She looked up at me with the same look in her eyes that Tara had five years earlier. But it wasn't the look of wanting to give me a blow job. It was the look of wanting me to kiss her. I didn't know what to do. I was too nervous to go in for a kiss, and I also was scared that if I moved my boob, sweat would leak and drown her. So instead I just smiled back at her and then looked back up at the TV. It was at that moment I knew I had friend-zoned myself.

Later that night she fell asleep next to me, and I felt butterflies. I had never spent the night at a girl's house, and even though we were just friends, I wanted to curl up next to her like a puppy and listen to her breathe. I turned off the TV and grabbed a blanket, and I laid it on top of her, making sure to cover every inch of her sweet cold little body. Then I lay down beside her and just watched her. I watched her sleep for hours, and I promise it's not as creepy as it sounds. I was just falling in love with this girl who I had been spending so much of my time with.

The next morning I heard her wake up. I closed my eyes and pretended to snore, so she wouldn't know I was up all night staring at her. As I closed my eyes I heard her get up, and I felt her put her blanket over me. When she lay back down and went back to sleep I couldn't help but be overwhelmed with love. I had never had a girl treat me like that, let alone want to sleep next to me. Even during sleepovers as a kid I was the one that people would stay far away from, mainly because I peed the bed and spoke in tongues when I hit my REM cycle. But it's not my fault I had a small bladder and an overly religious upbringing.

The next night we decided to go to the mall. While we were walking around we came across a Hot Topic store, and she dragged me in. Back in 2010 I had my own line of shirts in Hot Topic and they were as embarrassing as you'd expect. Lots of weird images of my face, way too many colors, and one shirt that said "SHANE DAWSON IS MY BOYFRIEND." I'm not sure who thought that was a good idea, considering I was a twenty-two-year-old man and my audience was mostly twelve, but either way, I'm sure today there is a Goodwill with LOTS of "Shane Dawson Is My Boyfriend" shirts. She dragged me inside and ripped one off the wall.

YOUTUBE GIRL: I HAVE to get this!

As she turned around I saw that she was holding up the boyfriend shirt. My heart exploded. Was this her asking to be my girlfriend? Was this her telling me that I'm more than a friend? Was she the only person who had ever wanted to buy one in this store, because there were HUNDREDS left on the wall? All these questions were filling up my brain, and I couldn't even bring myself to respond. Luckily I was cut off by an employee.

HOT TOPIC GUY: Hey, those are 50 percent off clearance. If you want to just take it, I won't tell anyone. I'm kinda sick of looking at that guy's weird face.

ME: No, we're just looking.

HOT TOPIC GUY: Hey, you look familiar. Aren't you the kid from *Drake and Josh*?

ME: Drake Bell? No, but I do get that a lot.

HOT TOPIC GUY: No! Josh Peck! The one that use to be all super fat. Now he has that weird "I used to be fat" body.

ME: That's me!

Sometimes it's easier to just go along with it.

As we walked out of the Hot Topic with no pride left in my body and no money left in my wallet from all the shitty Shane Dawson shirts she made me buy, YouTube Girl turned to me and asked me a question I will never forget. And surprisingly, it wasn't if I was gay.

YOUTUBE GIRL: Do you want to meet my family?

ME: What?

YOUTUBE GIRL: I have to go back home to see them soon. Do you want to come with me?

ME: Ya! Sure!

YOUTUBE GIRL: Cool! I've been telling them so much about you. They can't wait to meet you!

My first thought was, "WE'RE GETTING MARRIED!" My second thought was, "Oh God, I hope she didn't tell them about how I like to eat things out of her trash."

A week later we were on our way to her hometown in the middle of the country, and I couldn't have been more excited to see where she came from. How could a girl so beautiful be so sweet and so down-to-earth? In the airport we were waiting to hear our plane board and I noticed she was on her phone texting someone. My first thought was: "Awwww, she must be telling her parents that we are on our way! I bet they are so excited! They are probably setting up a hummus platter!"

When I looked down at her phone I saw a kissy face emoji. I didn't get too paranoid because she could have sent that to her mother. It's not weird to do that, right? I used to send pictures of my boobs to my uncle all the time!

When we got off the plane her family ran up to us and it was like a scene in one of those Christmas movies. We all embraced and hugged for a solid five minutes. I hadn't felt this much family love in a long time. Not since Kelly Clarkson won *American Idol*.

YOUTUBE GIRL'S MOM: Shane, it's so nice to finally meet you! I've heard so much about you!
ME: Nothing bad hopefully!
YOUTUBE GIRL'S MOM: No! And you are definitely going to have to show us that butt trick you do when we get home!

Moms like ass play? Who knew?

· · ·

That night we had a family dinner, and we all sat around talking until one in the morning. It felt so comfortable and so right. I sat next to my dream girl and gave her looks throughout the night. At one point she even put her hand on my leg under the table to let me know I was doing a good job impressing the parents. After dinner it was time to go to bed, and I was shown to her old childhood bedroom. I felt strange about sleeping in the bed that she'd probably hit puberty in, but I guess it would have been more strange to sleep in the same room as her in her parent's house. It's not like we were going to do anything, though. We hadn't even kissed! I wasn't even sure if we were dating. I felt like we were friends with benefits, but not the sexual kind. It was more friends with benefits of helping each other pick out clothes and organize each other's closets. Now that I think about it, maybe I was her personal assistant? Either way, I wasn't getting any horseplay, and I was getting anxious about it.

That night I woke up and needed to get a glass of water. As I walked into the kitchen, I saw that her mother was sitting at the table looking at Twitter on her laptop and eating some leftover dessert. She was my soul mate.

YOUTUBE GIRL'S MOM: Hey, Shane. You're up late.

ME: Ya, just thirsty. What are you doing up?

YOUTUBE GIRL'S MOM: Just reading what all these kids are saying about my daughter.

ME: You actually read that stuff?

YOUTUBE GIRL'S MOM: Oh ya. I read everything. Sometimes I even reply.

ME: Even to the bad stuff?

YOUTUBE GIRL'S MOM: That's the best part! I scare the shit out of them and tell them I'm gonna file a lawsuit for harassment. There's nothing better than a little troll scared shitless.

Once again, my soul mate.

YOUTUBE GIRL'S MOM: So, you really like my daughter, don't you?

ME: Yes, ma'am.

YOUTUBE GIRL'S MOM: What are you gonna do about it?

ME: What do you mean?

YOUTUBE GIRL'S MOM: Seems to me she likes you too. But you guys
   are so far in the friend zone you're practically doing each other's
   toenails. Which, by the way, it wouldn't hurt you to do something with yours. Your toenails are so long they're scratching up
   my wood floors.

ME: You really think she likes me?

YOUTUBE GIRL'S MOM: I've never heard her talk about anyone the way
   she talks about you. You've just got to tell her how you feel.

ME: Thanks.

YOUTUBE GIRL'S MOM: You're welcome. Now, one question, how do
   you spell "douche nozzle"? I'm trying to reply to this dumb-ass
   kid and I've already used "ass hat" four times tonight.

The rest of the trip I tried to find a way to tell my friend how
I felt but I just couldn't do it. I was so scared of her rejecting me
and then I'd be stuck spending the rest of the week with her in her
childhood home. It had terrible Reese Witherspoon movie written
all over it. But on the flight back home, I decided it was the time for
me to speak up.

ME: Hey, I want to talk to you about something.

YOUTUBE GIRL: Is this about my little sister asking if you wear a wig?
   It's not your fault. It just looks kinda fake sometimes.

ME: No. It's about my feelings for you.

YOUTUBE GIRL: Oh.

Oh. Just oh? I could already tell this wasn't going to end in wed-
ding bells, but it was too late. I had to say it.

ME: I like you. A lot. And I just don't know what we are doing.

YOUTUBE GIRL: What do you mean?

ME: I slept with you. I met your family. I even stayed up all night talking to your mom.

YOUTUBE GIRL: Wait what? First of all, we didn't sleep together!

ME: Sorry, what I meant was I watched you sleep.

YOUTUBE GIRL: WHAT?!

Backpedal. Backpedal.

ME: I'm sorry. This is all coming out wrong. I just wanted to tell you that I see you as more than a friend.

DING DING. She was getting another text.

YOUTUBE GIRL: Just a second.

She looked down at her phone and started to reply. As she answered her text I started plotting ways to get out of this situation. Maybe I would open the emergency door and get sucked out? Maybe I would try to hijack the plane and get shot by the air marshal? Anything seemed better than sitting in awkward silence waiting to have my heart broken.

As she finished her text she looked up at me and put her hand on my shoulder.

YOUTUBE GIRL: Shane. I love you. I really do. But I love you like a brother.

And there it was. The phrase I had heard from pretty much every girl I had ever been friends with. Always a brother, never a lover. As the plane landed my eyes filled with tears. She hugged me tight to make sure I knew that she cared, but it didn't help. I felt terrible and all I wanted to do was run home and have my grandma wipe my ass. You know, home-style comfort.

We got in the car and we sat in silence the whole way home. After I dropped her off I went back to my place and relived the entire friendship over and over again in my head. I couldn't believe I had let myself believe there was actually a chance with this beautiful girl. How stupid could I be? Girls like this don't go for guys like me. They go for guys with calf tattoos and credit card debt.

In the middle of the night I got a text. I was expecting an apology or maybe even a love letter, but instead I got something alarming. It wasn't a text from her. It was a text from her mother.

TEXT FROM YOUTUBE GIRL'S MOM: Shane, are you by any chance at my
    daughter's house?? She's not answering her phone, and I'm very
    worried about her. She was supposed to text me when she got
    home safe.

I knew there was something wrong. She was not the type to ignore her mother. I put on my clothes and drove over to her house as fast as I could.

BANG BANG BANG. After hitting on the door as hard as I could, it slowly opened and there was my sweet little pony covered in blankets looking like a train hit her.

ME: Oh my God! What's wrong?
YOUTUBE GIRL: I don't feel good.

She started to cry and fell into my arms. I called her family right away and found out that she had a history of really intense panic attacks. They asked me to stay with her for the night, so I did. Even though I was upset, I couldn't let my friend down.

ME: I'm gonna stay here, ok? You go back to bed. If you need me, just
    let me know.

YOUTUBE GIRL: Are you sure?

ME: Hey, I'm not gonna leave you. I promise.

As I helped her into her bed I heard a beeping sound from downstairs. I walked into the living room and saw her phone flashing. I assumed it was her mother, but when I looked at it, the name was unfamiliar. It was a guy's name, and there was a heart emoji next to it. Now I felt like I was starting to have a panic attack. I didn't know what do to. Part of me wanted to ignore it and just get through the night, but another part of me wanted to know who she had been texting throughout our whole friendship. Curiosity got the better of me, and I decided to open the message. I scrolled up to the top, and it looked like the conversation had started around the time she and I started hanging out every night. I wish I had never looked.

GUY: Hey, you still hanging out with that guy that's in love with you or something?

YOUTUBE GIRL: LOL don't say that. He's nice.

GUY: Ya, but nice doesn't get the panties off does it haha

YOUTUBE GIRL: You are so lame haha

GUY: What you guys doing?

YOUTUBE GIRL: Just hanging out in my room. Wish you were here.

GUY: With him there?

YOUTUBE GIRL: No. lol just me and you. ;)

I shut the messages. I couldn't read anymore. My heart was crushed. This whole time I had thought maybe she was into me. Maybe I had a chance. It turns out I had just been playing a game of truth or dare with myself. The dare had been to fall in love with a girl who was way out of my league, but the truth was that she would never love me back.

YOUTUBE GIRL: Shane. Can you bring me some water?

As I heard her call me from the other room, I knew I had a choice to make. Was I going to leave and be angry at her, or was I going to forget about all the petty bullshit and help out a friend. I decided to do the latter. I grabbed her a glass of water and went to her room, where she was lying with a blanket over her head.

ME: Here you go.
YOUTUBE GIRL: Thanks. I don't know what I would do without you, Shane.

The harsh reality was that I wasn't sure we could still be friends. I still had so many feelings for her and I couldn't imagine just hanging out with her and watching TV anymore. I wanted to spend time with a girl who wanted more from me than just a shopping buddy. I wanted someone to kiss me, hold me, and maybe give me a blow job. And not out of pity.

That night, after she started feeling better, I gave her a hug and headed home. I didn't see her much after that and she knew why. As much as I wanted her to have feelings for me, the truth was she didn't and that was ok. I'd spent so much time being mad at her when in reality she just wanted a friend, and I was the asshole who wanted more.

Years later, I ran into her again and we had a nice long talk about everything that went down. I'm not going to lie; when I saw her again, a lot of feelings came back up. She was just as beautiful as I remembered. Unfortunately I was just as terrible with women as I remembered.

ME: So how you been?

YOUTUBE GIRL: Oh, you know, just working so hard my feet are gonna fall off.

ME: Hey! If they do, give them to me so I can sell them for glue!

Ya. Some guys never learn.

Word Vomit

About the Artist

KENZIE RUTLEDGE is twenty-one years old and comes from a town with a population of about three hundred cows . . . Artesia, New Mexico. She has always had an interest in art, so after graduating from high school she decided to take things further by attending Santa Fe University of Art and Design for two years. She is now living in El Paso, Texas, getting her cosmetology license, but she is always keeping her artistic side alive by doing various commissioned work, henna tattoos, and custom paintings. Someone she really looks up to and who has been her greatest inspiration is Timothy Trentham. You can contact her by email at zeerutledge@hotmail.com, or, to see more of her work, you can follow her on Instagram @kenziekins_.

It was a cold winter night in 2012, and I was standing outside on Hollywood Boulevard in my very unflattering underwear, covered in my own vomit. I know what you're thinking: "Wow, Shane! I didn't know you were such a party animal!" I'm not. I'm the opposite of a party animal. I'm a funeral person. I would much rather be surrounded by people crying while a dead person slowly decays in front of them than by a bunch of drunk people constantly asking me if I'm trans. I appreciate the compliment, but no, unfortunately God gave these hips to a man.

Covered in puke and blending in with the homeless people, I looked up at the sky and prayed that the Mayans were right. There's nothing I would have enjoyed more at that moment than to have been hit by a massive tidal wave and killed on impact. But before I go any further with this awesome image, let's go back to 2007, so I can really set the mood.

I was hanging out with my friend Kate, and we were trying to decide what to get for dinner one Friday night. I had been on a pretty intense diet for the last year and lost 150 pounds, so all I ever had a craving for was a baker's dozen of donuts and a horse trough filled with mac and cheese. You know, something sensible. Well, because I didn't want to die of a heart attack and because Kate's not a horse, we decided to go to a Mexican restaurant down the street from my house. After about three bowls of salsa I started feeling a little sick to my stomach. Obviously, three bowls of salsa isn't healthy for anyone, but my stomach was typically pretty indestructible. When you're raised by a woman whose specialty is "Lashotdogna" you develop a pretty strong gut.

When we got back to my house I knew there was something for sure wrong with me. I started to sweat and see double, which was terrible, considering we were watching a straight-to-DVD Hilary Duff movie and I could barely take watching it with single vision. Kate started to notice I was acting funny and not just reacting to the terrible performances.

KATE: Hey are you ok?

ME: I don't think so. Do you see two Hilary Duffs?

KATE: No, just her and her sister. But if you think they look alike, you
    might be having a stroke.

ME: Can you get my mom? I think there's something wrong.

My mom rushed into my room and immediately went into nurse mode. She's not a trained nurse, but she'd taken me to the ER enough times to know how to fake it. I could never convince her that I wasn't dying, I just LOOKED like I was dying. There's a difference.

MOM: Shaney Bird, what's wrong?! What can Momma do?! Do you
    need an ambulance?! Should I call 911?!

ME: No, please don't. The neighbors already hate us. The last thing
    I want to do is give them the satisfaction of thinking I'm dead.

MOM: Well, what's wrong? Is it your butt or your head?

She definitely hadn't ever heard that in the ER. She must have been going rogue.

ME: No, it's—

BARRRFFFFFFFFFFF. As I tried to finish my sentence I was interrupted by projectile puke SO chunky and fast moving it looked like someone had hooked up a hose to a bucket of spaghetti sauce. (I'm gagging as I write this. Sorry, I'm just way too good at describing gross stuff. You should hear me describe my poop. I'll give you a hint: I use LOTS of the same adjectives that would be used to describe a seven-layer cake. THICK.) As I set free my three bowls of salsa, Kate jumped in front of me to catch it so it didn't go on my computer desk. That's the sign of a true friend. Well, that and someone who will watch a straight-to-DVD Hilary Duff movie with you without judgment.

MOM: Honey, what did you eat?!

I couldn't answer because my mouth was still filled with thick, juicy, hot, garlicky . . . You know what? I'll stop.

KATE: We went to the Mexican restaurant down the street.
MOM: The one with a C rating??
ME: I thought that was an A in Spanish!
MOM: That makes no sense.
ME: And "Lashotdogna" does??

The next day I woke up with the smell of a C-rated restaurant in my mouth and the look of death on my face. As I made my way to the bathroom I stepped on my scale because that was part of my morning routine. Wake up, tuck my boner into my underwear in case my mom walks in, check my MySpace messages to see if Lori Beth Dinberg ever wrote me back, and then weigh myself to see if I'd maintained. To my shock and excitement, I had lost three pounds! Granted it was three pounds of vomit, but still! I hadn't lost three pounds overnight since my mom made tuna Casseralph, which was basically a casserole made from all the clearance items at Ralphs. I'll let you in on a little secret: tuna plus Cheerios is NOT GOOD.

Anyways, the rush I got from losing that much weight in one night was intoxicating. I was already not in a great place when it came to my health. I had lost so much weight so quickly by essentially starving myself . . . I hadn't eaten delicious food in a long time. I was bound to slip up and binge, so the only way to get rid of the guilt was to throw it up. Up until this point I hadn't forced myself to purge, but after that three-pound weight loss I decided that it was something I should try.

That night I decided to go out by myself and have a full-on eat-a-thon. I even wore my sweatpants to make sure I had plenty of room to fill up. Similar to how you get Hefty trash bags when you have a party so you have somewhere to put all the beer cans and red cups. Except my pants were the trash bag, and my body was the party. Luckily I was the only one invited, so I didn't have to shower.

I drove through my favorite fast-food joint, which I hadn't been to in a year. I could smell the fries from my car even before I got in line. I watched a family of six order one hundred dollars' worth of food and get six bags in return from the cashier, and I thought to myself: "Pussies. I'm gonna destroy them."

DRIVE-THRU LADY: What would you like?
ME: You might want to get a chair and a snack, ma'am. It's gonna be a while.

I laughed at my clever joke. She didn't. It was nine p.m. on a Saturday, and she was working at a fast-food restaurant where homeless people go to pee. Her humor was a little jaded.

ME: Ok, first I will get a number one with extra sauce.

DRIVE-THRU LADY: Ok, would you like that extra large?

ME: Do you have a glass guard to keep homeless people from stabbing you?

I laughed. She didn't.

ME: I will also have a number four, five, nine, ten, three, and an apple pie.

DRIVE-THRU LADY: Are you having a party?

I looked down at my stretchy pants and gave them a good snap.

ME: Oh ya.

The next stop on my chemical-filled fake-food rave was a park by my house. I stayed in the car, opened up the food bags, and let the smell take over and the heat fog my windows. People walking by probably thought there was a couple in the car having hot, steamy sex. Little did they know it was just me passionately devouring an order of nuggets and a fish sandwich.

As I finished the first bag of food I started to feel sick, but I didn't want to give up. These were not the pants of a quitter! Well, actually they were, considering every person over the age of eight who wears sweatpants in public has obviously given up on life.

After the second bag, I looked in the mirror and saw that I was dripping with sweat. I hadn't ingested food like this in more than a year, and I wasn't reacting well. If my body had been a movie theater playing a Rob Schneider movie and the food was the audience, they were about to walk out. This was *Deuce Bigalow 2* bad. I could feel my stomach bubbling, and I reached for an empty bag as fast as I could. Without going into detail again, let me just say the audience didn't walk out, they ran. And they were VERY angry and VERY offended at what they saw. After the first "walkout" I could tell that there were still a few moviegoers in the handicapped section that needed help getting out. I had never tried to make myself throw up before, and I was terrified. As I stuck my finger down my throat my heart started to race. I felt like a criminal. I started to cry, and I couldn't stop. The reality of the situation hit me. I was becoming . . . bulimic. Something I never thought would happen to me. I wasn't a supermodel; I was a guy who shopped at Target and played UNO on Friday nights. The only things I'd ever purged were people from my friends list when they start posting about their new baby cousins they'd just met. We get it, you're single and can't find someone to have your own baby with so you have to shove someone else in my face. DELETE.

This is when I realized that bulimia wasn't just a disease for supermodels. It was a disease that didn't have a dress code. No matter what you looked like or who you were, you could have it and get trapped in its ugly claws. And now that I was there, it was frightening. After forcing myself to throw up I wiped away the tears and drove home faster than I ever had before. I stopped at a Dumpster and threw away the evidence, hoping I would never have to go through this again. I walked into my house and my mom asked me where I had been. I lied to her. I hadn't lied to her in years.

ME: I was at Target. Just looking around.
MOM: Oh, that sounds fun.
ME: No. It wasn't. It was horrible.

I started to cry and ran to my room. My mom must have known something was up because I LOVE Target and it has never let me down. Not even when they decided not to sell my last book, *I Hate Myselfie*, but I AIN'T BITTER! I went into the bathroom and looked at my reflection. I was covered in sweat. My mouth was outlined red from all the acid. My face looked puffy and full. I made a promise to myself that I would never do that again. I'd worked so hard to get my weight off and I didn't want to do anything that could hurt my body. The promise was genuine, and I felt 100 percent confident.

Until the next morning when I woke up and saw that I'd lost another two pounds. I instantly forgot all the events of the night before and felt a rush from seeing the number on the scale drop again. This marked the beginning of a five-year struggle with bulimia and never letting anyone in my life know about it. My mom must have thought I was going broke from all my trips to Target. Little did she know that "Target" was code for fast food and "a big sale" was code for LOTS of vomit.

Over the next five years I would binge and purge at least three times a week, and every time I had the same guilty feeling, and I would cry over the sink while looking at myself in the mirror. I would have the same conversation with myself.

ME: I promise I'm never ever doing this again. This is the last time. I'm done.

And then the next night I would drive by 7-Eleven and see they were having a sale on supersize pizza sticks, and all promises would be broken. The number of times I purged while all my friends were over at my house was insane. I would run to the bathroom and pretend I had diarrhea and none of them ever questioned it. Looking back, I feel like someone should have at least said, "Damn, Shane, is your ass ok?!"

When my ex-girlfriend Lisa and I started going out I was worried that she would suspect something, but she never did, despite some very close calls. One of which brings me back to the cold night in 2012 when I was wearing my underwear on Hollywood Boulevard, covered in my own puke.

It was the first time I was going to spend the night at Lisa's place, and I was terrified. What if I snore? What if I fart? What if I sleepwalk and try to choke her to death? Hey, you never know.

That night we had a big meal. Feeling like a failure, I planned to binge as much food as I could inhale, throw it all up, and pretend like it had never happened. This tactic, of course, made no sense because (1) you never get rid of all the food, (2) your body keeps 70 percent of the calories even if you puke it up instantly, and (3) bulimia actually makes you gain weight in certain circumstances, because your body is in a constant state of survival mode, so anything you eat and don't throw up your body takes and stores instantly.

The weight loss I had experienced five years prior had stopped shortly after I became bulimic, but I couldn't stop. It was like a drug. The high I got from bingeing and purging was pure ecstasy. Of course, just like drugs, with the highs came the lows, and man, were they low. Covered-in-vomit-on-a-street-corner low.

LISA: You ready for bed?
ME: Ya! I'll be right there.

Lies. I wasn't ready for bed. I was going to lie there till she fell asleep and then get up, hit four fast-food drive-thrus, and come back home to puke it all up. Wow, what a catch.

As I lay down next to her she wrapped her arms around me. It was romantic and sweet, but all I could think of was "GET YOUR FUCKING ARMS OFF ME I HAVE A 5-POUND BURRITO TO EAT!" How was I supposed to sneak out if she was all over me? Didn't she know I had business to take care of? Oh wait, of course not, because she wasn't insane like me and wasn't thinking about what it would taste like to put a Twinkie in a hot dog bun at two a.m.

As she fell asleep I slipped out and put on my shoes. I didn't even waste time putting on pants because I was going to be in my car anyways. As I walked to my car I started to get that high feeling. I was thinking about all the food I was going to devour and how good it was gonna feel as it went down. Of course I wasn't thinking about how horrible it would feel coming back up, but that's because when you are in that state your brain doesn't let you. That's why it's such a dangerous disease.

After my four drive-thrus I made it back to the parking space outside of Lisa's apartment building and started steaming up the car again. Four empty bags later it was time to fill them back up, if you catch my drift. After I filled them up I took a trash bag out of my glove compartment—I had really thought this through—and I threw them all in there. I hopped out of my car with a trash bag full of vomit and walked to the Dumpster in the back. As I made my way up I noticed that it was locked. Plan B. There was a bin at the top of Lisa's stairs where everyone in her complex would throw their trash if they didn't want to walk all the way down to the Dumpster. The image of me walking up the stairs with a bag of puke behind my back in the middle of the night reminded me of Santa Claus delivering presents to all the little children. Except instead of presents it was vomit, and this situation was about as far from merry as you could get.

As I walked up the stairs I tripped over my own foot, and what happened next was the worst thing I could have ever imagined. No, I didn't break my neck. It was worse. The bag of vomit ripped open and went all the way down the stairs and into the street. And it was all leading from Lisa's front door!

I started to panic. It was two a.m., and I was in my underwear, covered in my own puke—and it was a Saturday night, so people were bound to walk up and see me. Santa never had to deal with this shit, that fat lucky fuck!

I pulled myself together and decided I had to clean up all the evidence, so I tiptoed into Lisa's apartment and grabbed as many paper towels as I could find. I prayed to God she wouldn't wake up because I had no idea how I was going to explain this to her.

"Oh hey, Lisa! I was just vomiting all over your apartment complex and decided to clean it up at two a.m. You having good dreams?! Make sure to write them in your journal so you don't forget them!" What a disaster.

For the next three hours I was on my hands and knees cleaning up puke. I had to clean from her front door all the way to the street corner, where cars zoomed by honking at me. Drivers must have either thought I was a drunk or a really sad prostitute who had just given up on trying to look sexy.

While I was cleaning up my mess, I had another conversation with myself. This time, it was real.

ME: This is it. This is the last time. I'm never going to do this again. I promise. I know I've said this a million times before. But this time I mean it. I don't want to live like this. I don't want to have to lie to people I love and pretend like my ass is always leaking. I don't want to end up dead in a bathroom someday because my heart gave out. I just want to be healthy. I want to be happy. Please God, help me.

I took a shower and threw out my clothes and crawled back into bed with Lisa. She rolled over and opened her eyes.

LISA: You smell like barf.
ME: You're dreaming. Go back to sleep.
LISA: You're so weird. Love you.

That was the last time I ever wanted to lie to her or anyone else in my life. I decided to get help, so I started seeing a therapist and got my life together. It's still a daily struggle and I haven't been perfect. At least once a year I slip up, but I'm honest about it. I tell my therapist and my friends. Bulimia is a disease, and I knew I couldn't get over it alone. I'm so glad I ended up on that street corner covered in vomit because if I hadn't, I might be dead now. Or worse, a friend might have actually called 911 because they thought my asshole was gonna fall out. Seriously, how come NO ONE questioned that? Or maybe they knew the whole time I was struggling and were too scared to ask me about it.

A word of advice to anyone who thinks someone in their life is struggling with an eating disorder. Talk to them. Tell them not to be ashamed and that you are there for them. They might deny it, but it will open the door for them to come to you later when they are ready. Another word of advice. A Twinkie in a hot dog bun is NOT GOOD. Holy God. I might puke again just thinking about it. But don't worry, if I do, I won't describe it to you. I promise. And nowadays I keep my promises.

My Craigslist Hookup

About the Artist

MICAELA HORNING is from a small town in Wisconsin. She is currently eighteen years old and studying graphic design at her university with the hope of graduating with a BFA in graphic design and interactive media with a concentration in design. Her love of drawing stems from her childhood and the constant support and wonderful upbringing that her parents have given her. She hopes to someday create concept art for television, movies, and video games as well as possibly to be an illustrator or a tattoo artist.

It was the middle of the night, and I was standing on top of a shit-stained toilet, staring out the broken window of a dirty motel bath-room. As the wind blew through my hair I could smell weed burning and definitely some kind of animal giving birth. I heard a gunshot, then a scream, then a woman crying, and then silence. Before I could process the murder I just witnessed, I was distracted by a beat-up car pulling into the parking lot with a bumper sticker that said "DOWN TO POUND." My Prince Charming had arrived. I never expected my life to end up this way. Well, I did expect to be twenty-six years old, hovered over a motel toilet with someone else's turd floating in it, but I never expected to be waiting for a Craigslist hookup.

Before I came out as bisexual I had only ever been with women, and I was always too scared to try anything with a guy, even though I wanted to. I never went to college, so I kinda missed out on my experimentation days. Instead I had chosen to cross-dress on the internet in front of my webcam for children, which, now looking back, I guess is pretty experimental. Now that I was newly single I was ready to dip my toe into the gay pond and see if it turned pink. Would I like gay sex the way I liked straight sex? Would I hate it the way I hated watching my parents have sex? Would I feel nothing like the way I feel nothing when people ask my opinion on politics? Many questions left to be answered.

My main issue with finding a guy to have sex with was that I wasn't just a normal guy in the closet. I was a semi-kinda-but-only-online-famous guy in the closet. If I were to go out on a date with a guy in public and a fan saw us, it would turn into a scandal on Twitter, and the last thing I needed was another Twitter scandal. I'd already accidentally tweeted a picture that had a reflection of my junk in it, and that was a nightmare. Most of the people that watched me online assumed I was gay anyway. The closet I was hiding in wasn't even a closet; it was more like a beaded curtain. Pink, glittery, loud hanging beads just waiting for me to pop out and say, "HEY, QUEEN!!" Even though it wouldn't have been a shock to my audience, I still wasn't ready to publicly talk about it, so I had to take matters into my own hands.

First I tried Tinder because I figured maybe people in my area weren't updated on their YouTubipedia and would just think I was another sad single guy with way too many pictures of dogs on his profile. Seriously, what's with that? As I swiped through my options I saw the same types of pictures on every profile.

1ST PROFILE PIC: Guy looking serious while sitting at a bar.

2ND PROFILE PIC: Guy crouching down on the floor putting his face next to a dog that doesn't belong to him.

3RD PROFILE PIC: Guy who is shirtless but laughing about it 'cause it's like sooooo lame and he's sooooo self-aware.

4TH PROFILE PIC: Guy with a baby. No caption. No explanation. Just a baby.

LAST PROFILE PIC: DISNEYLAND. I have no idea what the fascination is with Disneyland, but it made me want to climb to the top of Cinderella Castle and jump off. Hopefully crushing a Mickey-ears-wearing gay dude taking a selfie.

After swiping over a hundred guys whose bio said, "How come nobody writes back on here??!" I finally had a match. He was an attractive guy who surprisingly wasn't holding a baby and wasn't wearing a shirt that said "My Disney Princess name is Taco Belle." I'm not kidding. I actually saw a guy wearing that. It made me want to "Crunchwrap" my hands around his neck and choke him to death. But the guy I matched with didn't look like the kinda guy I wanted to kill. He looked like the kind of guy I wanted to have anonymous sex with and then never call back.

DING!

I got a text, so I closed the app and opened the message. What I saw only made me feel even more helpless.

FRIEND: Shane! You just matched with my gay friend on Tinder! You're GAY?!?!

And then there were about five peach emojis and an eggplant. My heart broke. The second I thought I had found a potential date I was outed. It was going to be impossible to date privately. I deleted my Tinder app and decided it was time for something sneakier and potentially creepier. I recalled a conversation I'd had a few years before with a fellow YouTuber named Tyler Oakley, and if you don't know him, then you must live under a rock. A rock that has incredible sound protection, 'cause that motherfucker is LOUD. And it's not just his laugh that's loud; it's everything about him. From the pink hair to the tie-dyed reindeer head on his wall, the guy has no problem being himself, and I was always so envious of that. One night we were hanging out, and he referenced an app that I had never heard of. The conversation got real weird real quick.

ME: What's it called?
TYLER: Grindr! You've never heard of it?
ME: No. Is it like FatBooth? 'Cause I LOVE FatBooth! Or Ugly-

Booth?! Or OldBooth?! Or fat ugly old nasty acne cross-eyed dumb stupid bitch booth?!

TYLER: You use all those?

ME: I have a lot of issues. Back to Grindr.

TYLER: Ok, so Grindr is an app that tells you where all the guys are in your area that wanna hook up!

ME: Oh! So it's like Yelp! But for penis!

TYLER: Kinda. Except you don't leave reviews, and you NEVER return to the same restaurant or else you're actual gutter trash.

ME: Totally. One time I went to the grossest Chipotle and the guy serving me left an arm hair in my guacamole, and I left such a mean review. And then I went back the next week 'cause the only other Chipotle was like twenty minutes from my house.

TYLER: Ya, it's totally like that. Except not at all, and I think I'm gonna narf.

ME: Have you ever used it?

TYLER: A lady never tells her secrets!

ME: I wish someone would tell that to my mom. She recently told me that when she gave birth to me, she shit on my head.

TYLER: You make me sad.

So I deleted my Tinder account and decided to download Grindr. As the app loaded it asked me to enter my name. I obviously wasn't going to give them my real name, so instead I made up something cute and sexy that I had seen work in the past.

Name: *Taco Belle*

Perfect. Then it asked for a picture. I didn't want to show my full face obviously, and I didn't want to show my body because . . . obviously. So I just posted a picture of my mouth. In hindsight that was probably the wrong move, but I was nervous and wasn't thinking clearly. I even added a joke under my name that I thought was funny but then later realized how disgusting it was.

Bio: *Just a bean and cheese princess awaiting her extra spicy beast.*

Ya. I was just asking to get raped. So after I submitted my info, the app took me to what looked like a tic-tac-toe board, but instead of Xs and Os, there were dick pics and LOTS of nipple hair. There were over one hundred guys in a ten-mile radius of me, and the second they saw my mouth pic I had five messages. I was so overwhelmed. I saw words I didn't recognize, like "BTM" and "VERS." I saw pictures of the insides of guys' asses, which were surprisingly cleaner than I expected. I had only ever seen the inside of my own ass when I was twelve, using my mom's makeup mirror. I still can't believe she never got pink eye.

I finally got to a message that caught my eye. It was from a guy whose name was "Bob," and he seemed relatively normal. Granted, his face wasn't in his profile pic, but hey, neither was mine. Maybe he was a YouTuber in the closet too?! Maybe they were ALL YouTubers in the closet! I'm pretty sure there are hundreds of them. I opened his message and initiated some casual small talk.

TACO BELLE: Hi! I'm really scared and I've never done anything like this before because I'm in the closet and I'm not even sure if I'm gay or not. I actually think maybe I'm bi but I'm not sure if that's real because I feel like maybe it's my Christian guilt making me want to eat pussy. Like maybe I don't actually like it? Maybe GOD is making me like it?? KNOW WHAT I MEAN?!

Ya. Super smooth.

BOB: Calm down, man. Everything's ok. What's your name?

TACO BELLE: I can't tell you my name 'cause if you have teenage kids they probably know me, and then what if they find out you had sex with me?! What if you brought them to VidCon and when I gave them a hug they whispered, "I know you fucked my daddy" in my ear?!

BOB: I don't know what half of those words mean. What's VidCon?

TACO BELLE: I'm sorry. I'm just so nervous.

BOB: It's ok. I was nervous when I was young too.

TACO BELLE: Thanks. How old are you by the way?

BOB: 75. But I look 70.

FUCK. He was old enough to be my grandpa and was staring at a picture of my mouth, fantasizing about putting his shriveled old dick in it! This was too fucked-up even for me. Except he had been so nice to me that I couldn't just block him. So I decided to let him down easy.

TACO BELLE: I HAVE TO GO BYE!

Whew. Close call. Nice guy though. I hope he's not dead. Then I read the next message, from a guy named "Paul," and it seemed a little more my speed.

PAUL: Hey. Looking to try out guys on the down low. You down?

TACO BELLE: Ya! You're not gonna film it, right?

PAUL: What?

TACO BELLE: I don't know. I feel like people film sex a lot. I don't have it often, but I see so much porn online of people having sex and filming it on their iPhones and that's like my nightmare. The iPhone camera is SO unflattering.

PAUL: I have to go bye.

Damn. Instant karma. Oh well. Then I got a message that I will never forget.

NO NAME: Oh hey. You live in the same building as me.

WHAT?! How does he know that? Then I looked at his profile and saw that his current location was three hundred feet from me. OH MY GOD. He could see where I was! What if he was a serial killer? What if he was a neighbor I had ridden the elevator with? What if he was that annoying lady who has twenty dogs to fill the void in her heart from not having a husband?! What if THIS was what she did for fun? Find young guys and feed them to her dogs?? My mind was racing.

NO NAME: You got a nice mouth. I bet you really know how to use it.

HOLY SHIT! His current location was 200 feet away! He was getting closer!

ME: I'm sorry! I'm not interested!
NO NAME: You sure?

PICTURE SENT. I opened it, and it was the creepiest man chest I had ever seen. His chest hair was long enough to braid, and his nipples looked like they were crying!

ME: No! I'm sorry! Please stop talking to me!

Fifty feet away.

ME: PLEASE LEAVE ME ALONE!!!!!

Thirty-five feet away.

NO NAME: What are you talking about? I didn't say anything.

Ten feet away.

ME: PLEASE!!!!!! I DON'T WANT TO DIE!!!!!!!!!

Five feet away.

I dropped my phone and stood up from the couch. I started to breathe heavily. I imagined him standing on the other side of my front door with his shirt off and his nipples crying all over my welcome mat. I slowly walked over to the door, each step I took more terrifying than the last. I made my way to the peephole and slid it open. I put my face against the hole and I saw . . . nothing. Then I heard noise coming from above me. Keys rattling and a door opening. He lived ABOVE ME. He wasn't stalking me. He was probably coming home from work and was trying to get a little action on the way. I felt like such an asshole.

ME: I'm sorry. I thought you were stalking me lol.
GRINDR TEAM: You have been blocked from talking to No Name.

Andddddd time to delete Grindr. Which meant there was only one other place to find a potential hookup. Not a bar, or a mall, or a sexually open church. No, no, no, those all made way too much sense. It was time for me to go to Craigslist.

As I opened up Craigslist I had flashbacks of my mom and I shopping for a couch. Little did I know, twenty years later I would be shopping for someone to eat my ass. But hopefully they also had a couch. Hooking up in bed with a stranger you met on a website is a little tacky.

As I scrolled through the list of ads I noticed that they all had very similar headlines, most of which started with "NO AIDS." I'm gonna be honest though, NO AIDS was a plus. One ad stuck out, and I opened it.

SUBJECT: NO AIDS. LOOKING FOR DISCREET WITH A FIRST TIMER

Hey, my name is Greg. I'm a 6ft nice guy who likes helping straight guys figure out if they are interested in men. It's like I'm giving back to the universe. But with my dick. If you are a straight guy and want to see what you've been missing then hit me up for some animal style sex. Don't worry, I don't bite. Unless you want me to. ;) But I probably won't because that's one of the ways Aids is spread.

For some reason I thought this ad was a winner. Probably because I had already been through a night of getting caught by a friend and almost getting murdered by a guy whose body looked like it was a jar of old mayonnaise that started growing hair. I texted Greg and we started planning on where we were going to meet up. I hadn't thought it through this far. I didn't want to go to his place because what if he was secretly filming everything, and I didn't want him to come to my place because what if he recognized it from my videos and told everyone he fucked Shane Dawson? Worse than that, what if he knew I was a YouTuber but didn't remember my name and then after we had sex, said: "Oh, WAIT! Now I remember! You're Fred!"

I would kill myself. Right there. Right in front of him. Luckily I figured out a solid plan B. I would find a cheap motel, get a room, and wait for him with a knife under the bed just in case. Ya, that seemed like the perfect place to lose my butt virginity. Romance was in the air.

DING.

A text from Greg popped up on my phone.

GREG: Hey. I'm on my way to the motel. You hungry? I was gonna stop by In-N-Out.

Awwwww, he was offering to bring me food? This is third-date material! Maybe this would be the guy of my dreams?

GREG: Also, are there water bottles in the room? I need to douche.

And my dreams are over.

GREG: If you already used one on yourself, that's fine. I can just wash off the tip.

Nightmare. Actual nightmare. Shit-covered nightmare.

At the motel, I wanted to make sure he wasn't a murderer, so I stood on the toilet and stared out the window. I stood there with the cold wind freezing my face for at least an hour. Why would he pick In-N-Out? Doesn't everyone know those lines are ridiculous? And for what? A burger in a box instead of a bag? Get over yourself.

Then I saw his car pull up. My heart started pounding so hard my body was shaking. I was more nervous than I'd ever been in my life, and I couldn't think straight. As he got out of his car, I realized that he wasn't really my type and I wasn't even sure what my type was. I just knew it wasn't a huge hairy dad with neck tattoos spelling out the names of his dead wives. Most likely that he killed. I started to panic. This was just like the Grindr experience but worse because I couldn't just delete the app! The guy knew where I was and was walking up to my room! Even worse, he was holding a box of

In-N-Out. Really, dude? You were gonna fuck me while the smell of pickles and onions filled the room? I know your ad said you were into "animal style," but this was a little much.

As he walked up the stairs I began to plan my escape. Maybe I could jump out the window? Maybe I could play a gunshot sound effect on my phone, and he would think I shot myself? And that would be pretty normal for the neighbors. I'm sure someone killed himself in this motel at least twice a week.

KNOCK KNOCK.

Shit. It was too late. I walked up to the door and put my ear to it.

ME: Hi.

GREG: Hi! Can I come in now? My fries are leaking.

His fries were leaking? What did that even mean?? You had sauce already on your fries before you were even at the table? What kind of person does that? A fucking sicko, that's who.

ME: I'm sorry. I can't do this. Please don't be mad.

GREG: Let me in, man. Let's talk about this.

ME: I can't. I'm too scared. And I just want to go home.

I started to cry. I was so overwhelmed with emotion that I couldn't hold it in any longer. Nobody else I knew had had to go through this. None of my friends had had to find a stranger to have anonymous sex with to figure out their sexuality. They just went to bars and met people like normal human beings. Not hide in the shadows while the smell of secret sauce filled the room.

GREG: Hey, man. You really have never done anything with a guy?

ME: No. That's why I answered your ad. To see if I was gay. Or bi.

Or whatever.

GREG: Can I give you some advice?

ME: Sure.

GREG: I know you wanted to do this to see if you were interested in sex with men but . . . if you were looking for it in the first place . . . you were interested. You don't need to have sex to realize that, man. Just live your life and do it when you're ready.

Of course he was right. I'd suppressed my attraction toward men for so long. For some reason I thought that since I was ready to try it out, I needed to just have sex with the first man I could find to make sure the feelings were real. But of course they were real. That's why they're feelings. My heart had known the truth all along, and I didn't need to have sex to prove it.

GREG: Good luck, man. You're gonna be fine. Just look how I turned out!

Not a great example, but I was still appreciative. As he walked away, I sat on the motel bed and considered how far I'd come. And it was far. I used to be a kid who was terrified to admit that he liked boys, and here I was a guy who had been just about to have sex with a guy he met online. As creepy as it sounds, I was proud of myself. I knew that the first time I hooked up with a man I actually cared about would be just as amazing as the first time it had been with a woman I cared about. After I came out all bets were off, and it was time to go out and live my life. And without getting too graphic, I did find a guy to be with, and it was amazing. Definitely more amazing than it would have been with Greg from Craigslist. No offense, Greg.

The White Bus

About the Artist

PAIGE RHOADS is an aspiring artist from Topeka, Kansas, and is currently attending school at Emporia State University. She has known art was her calling since she was very young. She mainly sticks with paintings, but dabbles in other mediums, too. To see her collection of work, visit paigerhoads .weebly.com.

There's nothing harder than having to move to a different school and start all over again. You put so much time and energy into making friends, building a routine, learning which teachers are easiest to emotionally break, and then one day you are forced to go to another school and start all over again. It's what I assume dating on Tinder is like. You talk to a stranger for a few days and then they just stop replying after all that effort you put into the relationship. That's why I would much rather be alone forever and occasionally bump into strangers in a crowded department store so I can get a sense of human touch. Ya, way healthier.

Anyways, the summer after fourth grade we moved to a different town and into a much smaller house. It was the hottest summer in ten years, and I tried everything in my power to stay cool. In the past, I had just gone over to my neighbor's house to swim, but now that I didn't live next door anymore, I had to get creative. One scorching hot day I decided to pull the big trash can from the front of my house to my backyard and fill it with hose water. I got a step ladder and then jumped inside. Not only did I barely fit, but all the dried-up sludge and dead bugs splashed into my mouth. It was pretty much the opposite of refreshing. Even sadder, I stayed in it for two hours.

It was during hour two that my brother zoomed into the backyard on his bike, saw me floating in a city trash can filled with sewage, and busted up laughing.

ME: I was just cleaning it!
JERID: In your swim trunks?

I tried to jump out but caught my leg on the side of the can, and the whole thing tipped over and tidal waved onto the driveway. I tumbled out covered in brown slime and slapped my head pretty hard on the ground. My brother laughed so hard I'm pretty sure he popped a blood vessel in his head. That or he had been smoking a lot of weed, which now that I think about it actually makes sense. I can't imagine being high and then seeing your fat little brother sitting in a trash can full of water looking like a pig in a Crock-Pot. I bet it was comedy gold. After I got up and spit garbage juice out of my mouth, my brother sat down on the patio and told me to come join him for a talk. Our talks were usually father-son type chats. My dad wasn't really around much, so Jerid was who I would go to for advice. Usually it was bad advice, and sometimes he would just ask me to cover for something bad he had done, but I still treasured these moments.

JERID: So, you nervous about the new school?
ME: A little bit. I'm more nervous about people thinking I'm deaf.

My new elementary school was Helen Keller Elementary. I completely understand why a school would be named after her. She was a true hero and deserves to be honored. But is it really fair to the kids who go there? Every time someone would ask my mom what school I was transferring into they would respond with a look of deep sympathy and concern. She had a conversation with her boss once that took a pretty dark turn.

MOM'S BOSS: Which school does he go to?
MOM: Helen Keller Elementary.

MOM'S BOSS: Oh, you poor, poor thing. I can't imagine how hard it is to have a child with disabilities.

MOM: Oh, no, it's not—

MOM'S BOSS: And to top it off, he's overweight? You deserve a gift for how much you have to put up with.

MOM: Actually—

MOM'S BOSS: When was the last time we talked about giving you a raise?

My mom paused and put on a fake sad face.

MOM: You don't know pain until you've come home to see your fat deaf blind son floating in a trash can full of water because he thinks it's a swimming pool.

MOM'S BOSS: You poor thing!

Ya, after that exchange, every time I saw that boss I had to pretend to bump into walls. My mom bought me a Furby with her bonus check, so I guess it was worth it.

Day one at my new school was pretty terrifying, but what was even more terrifying was that it was the first time I had to walk to get there. I lived close enough that I didn't need my mom to drop me off, but I had never done it before, and I was scared that someone might try to kidnap me. Then I remembered I wasn't really kidnapping material. Why would a child molester want a two-hundred-pound ten-year-old who had more armpit hair than he did? So I guess I was pretty safe. As I walked into the gates I saw kids playing four square and girls jumping rope like professionals. I even saw a teacher bandaging up a student's scraped knee. It was like I had walked into a 1950s commercial for the perfect elementary school. Then a ball flew at my face, and all the kids screamed, "Ten points for the whale hit!" Commercial over. Reality checked.

The bell rang, and I walked into my new classroom. I looked around the room and found a seat close to the back. I never liked to be near the front because I was afraid the teacher would call on me. I had a huge fear of public speaking, and the last thing I wanted to do was have people hear what my voice sounded like. Sometimes I wished it really was a school for the deaf and blind because then I would feel WAY more comfortable.

The teacher introduced herself, and I should have known this year was going to be a weird one. She had bloodshot eyes, and her face looked red and puffy like she had been up all night crying.

MRS. COLDWATER: Hello, students, I'm Mrs. Coldwater. Well, not anymore technically. After last week I guess I should change it back to my maiden name. So THAT'S WHAT I'M GOING TO DO TODAY.

She grabbed a piece of chalk and pressed it deep and hard into the chalkboard and crossed out her name and wrote MISS FLETCHER over it.

MISS FLETCHER: PERFECT! Let's get started!

Ya, it was going to be a rough year. Lunchtime rolled around, and it was time to find a place to sit and eat my tuna salad sandwich. I don't know why my mom thought it was a good idea to pack a tuna sandwich into my backpack so it could get hot and stinky for half the day. Maybe she thought it would be a good conversation starter? Maybe I would open up my backpack, and a kid would smell the wretched stench that came from it and ask me what it was. Unfortunately that didn't happen. When I opened up my bag, everybody just looked disgusted and moved to another table. As I sat alone eating my Fancy Feast a girl came up to me and asked if she could join. She was an overweight Cambodian girl named Saksa, and she had the kindest eyes I had ever seen.

SAKSA: Hi. My name is Saksa.

ME: My name is Shane. You new here too?

SAKSA: Ya. What are you eating? It smells good.

ME: You think so? Most people think it smells like a prostitute's nail bed.

SAKSA: Well, my family usually cooks up a bowl of fish heads and blends them into a smoothie, so I'm not the best judge of smell.

ME: You drink that?

SAKSA: No, I usually drink chocolate milk. My grandma's a fan of things that smell like the dump.

ME: My grandma's a fan of taking dumps that look like chocolate milk, so I guess we have a lot in common!

After school I said good-bye to my new friend and started my walk home. It was then I saw a big white bus parked in front of the school. I saw a few kids going in, and they looked so excited. I overheard one kid say, "I hope they have Airheads today!" That was all I needed. I joined the line and pretended like I was a part of this mystery candy club. I stepped onto the large white bus and saw three men in their thirties walking around giving the kids hugs. The first thing I noticed was how fake their smiles looked. It was almost like they were robots and they were set on "way too touchy mode." The next thing I noticed was how long their neck hair was. It was literally long enough to comb. If they had put gel in it they probably could have spiked it. I wasn't sure who these guys were, but they smelled like Reese's, so I was in.

NECK-HAIR GUY 1: Welcome, kids, to the Lord's Bus!

Fuck. Wrong choice. Must find exit.

NECK-HAIR GUY 2: Who's ready for a game of "Who Wants to be a Bless-
  ingaire?" John, grab the bowl of Snickers!

I guessed I could stay for one round. The three neck-hair brothers started asking us kids questions about the Bible, and whoever
got it right got a candy bar and a blessing. I grew up religious and I
definitely loved me some Jesus, but "church people" really freaked
me out. There was something so phony to me about people who
quoted Bible verses as if they were rap lyrics. I could imagine Jesus is
up there going, "Whoa. Too much, guys. Chill."

It was my turn to answer a question and I was ready. I was pretty
sure I wouldn't get the answer right, but I'm sure if I looked sad
enough they would still throw me a Snickers. Kinda like how when
a whale at SeaWorld doesn't do the trick right but the trainer still
throws him a fish.

NECK-HAIR GUY 3: Ok! How many of each animal did Noah bring into
  the ark?
ME: Oh! I know this one! Two!
NECK-HAIR GUY 3: That's correct!!

He threw me a Snickers, which I caught in my mouth.

NECK-HAIR GUY 3: Aren't you going to unwrap that?
ME: Nah, I can do it with my teeth.

What can I say, I was a talented whale. At the end of the game
they sent us on our way, and I felt full of sugar and even more full
of bullshit. Some of the things these hairy-necked nerds were saying

were so out of touch I couldn't believe nobody was calling them out on it. I understood that a lot of people believe every word of the Bible, but from my point of view some of it was clearly outdated. I mean, it was written thousands of years ago. Some of my tweets from two months ago are outdated and need to be deleted. Imagine if Jesus was on Twitter. Do you think he would follow people? Or would we have to only follow him? Ugh, Twitter is SO confusing.

The next day after school I went into the bus again, and this time we were given an assignment.

NECK-HAIR GUY 1: When you go home today, try and make someone smile. Tomorrow come back and tell us what you did and how good it felt to make someone happy!

A sad-looking kid raised his hand.

NECK-HAIR GUY 1: Yes, Keith?

KEITH: If I don't go home that would make my mom smile. Does that count?

NECK-HAIR GUY 1: No. And also, you should stay quiet when you come to the white bus. You make us sad.

We all nodded in agreement. Later that night I went home and tried to think of something that would make my mom smile. It wasn't hard to do, but I wanted to make sure it was something good that would get me extra candy. I decided to draw her a picture and give it to her when she got home from her date. I tried my hardest to make it look just like her. I wanted to capture her essence. I wasn't the best artist, but it wasn't about that. It was about the effort and thought I was putting into it. Then my mom got home.

MOM: Why is every man on earth an asshole?!

I ran up to her with my picture, hoping it would cheer her up and turn her frown upside down.

ME: Mom! I drew you!

She looked at my drawing and started to cry.

MOM: THAT'S WHAT I LOOK LIKE?! No wonder no man wants me!!!

She ran into her room and slammed the door. I looked down at the picture, and after taking a second look I guess it did kind of look like a gremlin having a panic attack. I threw my picture in the trash, and as I headed to her room to comfort her I heard my brother run down the hallway.

JERID: OPEN NUTS!

He PUNCHED me in the dick, and I fell to my knees and screamed. He laughed hysterically and then continued on to the kitchen. It hurt like hell, but hey, I made him smile! And I also got hurt in the process. That must be worth a few extra fun dips!

The next day at lunch I told Saksa about the white bus.

SAKSA: So it's a big white bus full of grown men that give you candy?
ME: Yep!
SAKSA: You are aware of how creepy that sounds, right?
ME: Yep!
SAKSA: Right . . . so why do you go?
ME: Um, what part of it did you not understand? There's CANDY.
My mom doesn't keep candy in the house, so usually if I get a craving for sugar I just have to eat pancake batter.

SAKSA: Eww, doesn't that hurt your stomach?

ME: Saksa, when you got a stomach as strong as mine, nothing can hurt you. Last week I got a craving for something salty, so I ate a brick.

SAKSA: White people are crazy.

Over the next week I learned a lot on the white bus. That's a lie; I wasn't paying attention. But I did learn that I'm more of a chocolate guy than I am a sour guy. And that was honestly a big revelation for me. All those years I had thought my first choice would be Sour Patch Kids but then I realized God had a different plan for me. Peanut butter and chocolate. Praise the Lord.

Everything seemed to be going well until one day when the three brothers taught us a lesson about homosexuality being wrong. This was back in the nineties, so things were much different. There were many people who were outspokenly antigay, and most of them were coming from a Christian mind-set. Even at age ten, I knew something wasn't right.

NECK-HAIR GUY 1: And so that's why homosexuality is wrong. Does anyone have any questions?

ME: Ya, do gay people go to hell?

NECK-HAIR GUY 1: We aren't supposed to say that, but it does say in the Bible that if you disobey God and love the same sex then you will spend an eternity in the fiery pits of hell.

ME: It says that?

NECK-HAIR GUY 1: I paraphrased it a bit. Kit Kat?

That day I didn't feel like candy. I didn't feel like taking anything from them at all. I was starting to wonder if this bus was here to brainwash kids instead of giving them a safe place to go after school.

I thought talking to a group of ten-year-olds about homosexuality was incredibly over the line. But I was too scared to say anything, so instead I just waited until the discussion was over and got off the bus. As we walked out, the hairy boys yelled at us in unison.

NECK-HAIR GUYS: Tomorrow is Bring a Friend day! We'll have candy AND nachos!

Fuck everything I just said! They were gonna have NACHOS?? I decided I could put up with the prejudice for one more day. The next afternoon I convinced Saksa to come with me to the white bus. But it wasn't easy.

ME: Come on, please!
SAKSA: I don't know; they sound scary.
ME: They are. But not in a threatening way. More in a Michael's employee way.
SAKSA: I dunno.
ME: They are gonna have free nachos.
SAKSA: Who's got two thumbs and loves her some baby Jesus?! THIS GIRL!

That day after school Saksa and I made our way onto the bus, excited about the processed-cheese product to come. As we made our way to our seats the three hairy guys got in front of the group and introduced the day's topic.

NECK-HAIR GUY 2: I'm so happy so many of you brought friends! Now, who here is Christian?

Pretty much everyone except for Saksa raised their hands.

NECK-HAIR GUY 2: And what are you, miss?

SAKSA: I'm Buddhist.

NECK-HAIR GUY 2: Oh, that's nice. That man is so fun to look at! Like a big Beanie Baby!

NECK-HAIR GUY 3: Ooooooh, I LOVE Beanie Babies!

SAKSA: What did you just say?

NECK-HAIR GUY 2: I'm sorry. I didn't mean to offend you. Why don't you tell the group a little bit more about your religion?

SAKSA: Ok. What do you want to know?

NECK-HAIR GUY 2: Tell us what you believe in. What are some fun things you do to celebrate your god? We like to sing songs about Jesus and put on puppet shows.

SAKSA: Oh, well we don't really do that. But we do believe in reincarnation, which is pretty cool.

NECK-HAIR GUY 2: Tell us about that.

SAKSA: Well, basically it means that when you die you come back as someone else.

NECK-HAIR GUY 1: WOW! That sounds like a crazy movie!

All the neck-hair guys started to laugh.

SAKSA: It's not. It's what I believe in.

NECK-HAIR GUY 1: I know! I'm just saying, it sounds very fun! Almost like an episode of *Sabrina, the Teenage Witch*!

NECK-HAIR GUY 3: Ooooooh, I LOVE Sabrina!! That talking cat is HYSTERICAL!

SAKSA: NO! It's not a TV show. It's my religion!

Saksa started to get so frustrated I thought she was going to cry.

ME: Maybe we should change the subject. Who wants nachos?!

SAKSA: Fuck this. I'm out.

Saksa stormed off the bus. As I went to follow her one of the hairy-necked guys grabbed me by the shoulder.

NECK-HAIR GUY 1: You can be friends with her Shane, but just remember, everything she says is a lie. It's not her fault; it's her parents' fault for teaching her those things. But as her friend it's now your job to make her realize that Jesus is the only way.

ME: You know what, the only reason I started coming to this stupid bus was because you guys were passing out treats and had surprisingly comfortable seating for a bus, but I'm done. You know what I learned today?

NECK-HAIR GUY 1: That God works in mysterious ways?

ME: No, I learned that I know a lot more about God than you do. God doesn't judge. God doesn't make people feel bad for what they believe in. God doesn't care if you're gay or not. God is love. That's all he is. And I know God made all of us in his image, but he must have fucked up with you guys, 'cause you are the farthest thing from God I have ever seen.

I stormed off the bus and left those hairy freaks speechless. I caught up with Saksa, who was sitting on the street corner looking up at the sky.

ME: Hey. I'm sorry about those guys. I just told them off. It was awesome. I'm pretty sure they are gonna crash their bus into a gas station.

SAKSA: Cool.

ME: What are you looking at?

SAKSA: The sky.

ME: Trying to find clouds that look like penises?

SAKSA: No. Who does that?

ME: I dunno. NOT me.

SAKSA: Do you think it's all bullshit?

ME: Religion?

SAKSA: Ya.

ME: I dunno. I'm not sure which one is the truth. Or if any of them are. But I'm pretty sure there's somebody up there watching all the dumb shit we do and laughing.

She laughed. I'd made her smile. That time I didn't do it for the candy.

ME: Hey, we should make our own club.

SAKSA: What? The fat kids who will eat anything club?

ME: Whoa! You should join the psychic club, 'cause you just READ MY FUCKIN' MIND!

We laughed as we stared up at the sky. It was a moment I'll never forget. The first time I stuck up for a friend and also the first time I stuck up for myself. Maybe fifth grade wasn't going to be so bad after all.

ME: Seriously though, can we go to 7-Eleven and get nachos? It's all I can think about.

SAKSA: Totally.

Welcome to Mexico

About the Artist

ERIKA GRAPE has had a passion for art her entire life. She went to a fine arts–specialized high school and has big dreams. At the age of twenty-one, after a one-and-a-half-year detour to early childhood education, followed by some time at a university, she's beginning to pursue a creative career in the course of aiming for an art degree. Born and raised in a small Swedish town just outside of Stockholm, she is ready to make her own path in life and take on the world. Follow her everywhere @erikagrape.

W hen people ask me what my dream vacation is I always give the same answer: sleeping pills and a hole in my mattress that I can pee into. Traveling has never been a passion. There's nothing intriguing to me about packing up all my crap and sitting in a hot, sweaty death trap for five hours while hundreds of people fart simultaneously into sticky pleather chairs. I don't need to pay $500 for a plane ticket to sit in a room full of farts. I can just do that at home for the low cost of one Chipotle bowl.

One of the biggest differences between me and my last girlfriend, Lisa, was her love of traveling and my love of sitting on the couch all weekend twisting my pubic hair into small balls so they were easier to pull out. She should have known what she was in for on our first date when our conversation went a little something like this:

LISA: So, what's the one place you want to visit before you die?
ME: Wow, that's hard! I'd say it's a toss-up between the donut shop in Texas that puts the icing and sprinkles INSIDE the donut or the *Full House* house.
LISA: You're kidding, right?
ME: No! It's 100 percent real! I don't know how the icing and sprinkles don't completely disintegrate after being put in the deep fryer, but honestly, I've just decided to stop questioning shit. Life is just crazy, you know? Let's embrace it.

I go in for a cheers with my drink. She just stares at me confused for a good three minutes.

ME: Side note, do you think Kimmy Gibbler is based on a real person? And part two, who in your life do you consider to be a total Gibbler? Discuss.

Ya, my first-date conversation skills weren't great. But for whatever reason, Lisa didn't go to the bathroom and jump out the window. About a year into our relationship she asked me if I ever wanted to take a trip to Europe with her. I knew the correct answer was yes, but I didn't want to lie to her. It didn't sound fun to me. I don't have a problem with Europe or with going to other countries. My main problem is being trapped on a plane for ten or more hours having to watch shitty movies that literally nobody would ever choose to watch in the real world. I was once so desperate for entertainment on a long plane ride that I watched a documentary about people who were in love with inanimate objects. A lady married a roller coaster, and I actually cried. This is what planes do to me.

LISA: Come on! Let's go to Europe!
ME: I don't know. Can't we just find something cool to do around here?
LISA: Like what? The only thing close to us is the beach and you refuse to go there.
ME: It's not my fault! The sand freaks me out. Why is there SO much of it? And how long has it been there?! Like a million years? You know how gross that is?
LISA: This coming from a guy who asked me the other day what the purpose of shower soap was.
ME: What's the point of it when the shampoo is just going to drip down my body anyways?!
LISA: Please, let's just go! We can go to Paris and see the Eiffel Tower!

And then we can go to Amsterdam and see a sex show! And then we can go to Rome and see the ruins!

ME: What's a sex show?

LISA: It's a theater where there's a couple having sex onstage and the audience watches!

ME: Well, here in America we just call that porn, and we can watch it from the comfort of our own homes.

LISA: You watch porn?

ME: NO! NEVER! You're the only porn I need, baby!

LISA: Just tell me at some point we will leave the country together?

ME: Of course.

Two lies in a row. Not only did I have no intention of leaving the country, I also watched porn EVERY SINGLE NIGHT. But sometimes in relationships you have to tell a little lie to keep your partner happy. Or maybe you shouldn't do that and that's the reason relationships don't work? Whatever, I'm not a therapist.

So to my surprise, a year later we ended up taking a trip to another country, even though we weren't planning on it. Except it wasn't a trip as much as it was a horrible mistake that almost got us arrested and killed.

One weekend Lisa and I decided to go down to San Diego to visit some of her friends. I've always been a fan of San Diego, mainly because it is the mecca for Mexican food, since it is so close to the Mexican border. After a fun couple of days eating tacos and wandering around a cute little beach town we decided to get in our car and head back to Los Angeles. On the car ride back home we got into a really heated discussion that made us lose track of the direction we were headed. But we couldn't help it. It was a VERY serious debate.

LISA: No, he didn't!

ME: Yes, he did! The guy from *Blue's Clues* killed himself!

LISA: If he killed himself, I think more people would have heard about it.

ME: It was a cover-up! They replaced him with some random guy that looked nothing like him, and all the kids watching were too stupid to catch it!

LISA: That makes no sense. Why would he have killed himself anyway?

ME: One word: "illuminate."

LISA: What the fuck is that?

ME: Umm . . . only the biggest underground organization in the world that is controlling everything using their powers that they have gained through deals with the devil.

LISA: No, not that. The sign coming up!

We both looked straight ahead and didn't see the "Welcome to Los Angeles" sign we were expecting. Instead we saw something truly frightening.

ME: WELCOME TO MEXICO?!

That's right. We had gotten so engrossed in our *Blue's Clues* conspiracy theory that we didn't notice that we were going in the opposite direction. In the words of the country we were entering, this was NO BUENO.

LISA: Turn around!!

ME: I can't! All the cars are going in this direction!

LISA: Is there an exit?!

ME: Um, YES! The HUGE exit from America to Mexico!

LISA: Oh my God!

As we passed the Welcome to Mexico sign we saw a sea of taillights in front of us. There were huge lines of cars waiting to get through the border.

LISA: Oh no. We don't have our passports!

ME: Ok, don't panic! We can get through this! Remember that one time we went to Disneyland and they ran out of Fastpasses?

LISA: Shane, pretending you have a fake leg isn't going to help us in this situation!

ME: Well, do you have a better idea?!

LISA: Let's just say we got lost and want to go home.

ME: Do you WANT to get your head chopped off?

LISA: Ok, let's just talk to the person at the gate and maybe they will help us.

ME: Oh no.

LISA: What?

ME: My friend was in my car last weekend.

LISA: So?

You know how we all have that friend who is so full of pot that their body just leaks it? Well, that friend had been in my car the weekend before, and I was about 99 percent sure there were traces of marijuana in my backseat.

ME: There might be pot in the car.

LISA: Are you fucking kidding me??

I'd never wanted to be the guy from *Blue's Clues* more in my life. I was about to be trapped in Mexico with no passport, no money, and a car full of weed. I wished someone would kill me and replace me with a look-alike. But hoped he had good hair. My fear is that someone tells me I look like someone with a receding hairline.

LISA: Where's the pot?!

ME: I don't know! I just know she probably dropped some of it somewhere or hid it in a seat cushion.

LISA: Who the hell is this friend?! The fuckin' Easter bunny?!

We were next in line, and the gatekeeper waved us forward. It was the moment of truth. Time to act super casual and be really rational and explain that this was all just a giant misunderstanding.

GATE WOMAN: Next!

ME: Hi! We're Americans and we're scared!!

I instantly started bawling my eyes out.

LISA: What are you doing?!

ME: I don't know! I don't want to go to jail!

GATE WOMAN: Next!

ME: Wait, don't you want to check our passports? Or look in our car?!

Lisa punched me in the side to shut me up. The gatekeeper waved us through and didn't want anything to do with us. We got in with no problem! What a relief!

I pulled the car over, and we started laughing hysterically. All the adrenaline had caused us to go into some kind of insane mental state where everything was hilarious to us.

ME: Did you see how much I was crying?!

LISA: Ya! That was the most unattractive you've ever been to me! I would rather fuck my own brother than fuck you right now!

We laughed for a few minutes, and then reality set back in.

ME: Wait . . . how do we get out?

LISA: Well, we just go to the exit side of the border and tell them what happened. I'm sure they will just let us through. Just start crying again. You're good at that.

As I pulled the car back into the street I noticed a long line of cars that extended farther than the eye could see.

ME: Wow, I wonder what that line is for?

As I followed the line with my eyes I saw it led all the way up to where we were. And that's when it hit me.

ME: Oh my God. That's the line to GET OUT!

And in that moment it wasn't just me who turned on the water-works, it was both of us. Lisa and I started wailing like children who just got slapped in the grocery store for stealing too many grapes. I could barely understand what she was saying through all her tears and gasps.

LISA: That . . . line . . . is . . . gonna take . . . forever!

ME: And we're almost out of gas!! And our money doesn't work here!!!!

Not only were we trapped in Mexico with no passport and no money, we had about an hour's worth of gas left before we were totally stranded.

ME: Maybe the line goes fast?! Let's ask someone!

I drove over to another car near the front of the line. I asked the driver to roll down his window.

ME: Excuse me! How long did it take you to get to the front?

STRANGER: *Tres días!*

LISA: What did he say?

ME: I don't know. It sounded like "quesadillas."

LISA: Ask again.

ME: What??

STRANGER: *TRES DÍAS!*

LISA: Wow. He really is saying "quesadillas." How bizarre. Maybe it's slang here?

ME: English, please? Sorry, we're not from here!

A woman popped out from the passenger seat with a plastic fan in her hand, looking like she was near death.

WOMAN: He said THREE DAYS!

At that moment I could hear my heart stop beating. I turned to Lisa, and she was white as a ghost. We were screwed. The crying came back.

ME: It's gonna be ok! We can get through this!

LISA: How??

I looked around the exit of the border and noticed an empty lane next to the full one.

ME: Ok, let's go through that empty lane and just play stupid when we get to the gatekeeper.

LISA: I think that's a lane for cops only.

ME: Well, what's the worst that can happen? They aren't gonna shoot us!

LISA: How do you know that?

ME: Because cops are here to help us!

LISA: We're in Mexico.

ME: So?

LISA: You really need to read more.

I pulled my car into the cop line and drove up to the gatekeeper. Lisa grabbed my hand and gave it a kiss. My body started trembling with fear. I have never been good at breaking the rules. Even in school if a teacher told me I did something wrong, I would have a full-on panic attack. The thought of a cop yelling at me while holding a gun was making me borderline pee my pants. Pun intended. About that time, a cop approached my window.

COP: Are you aware that this is a police lane only?

ME: It is?! Whaaaaaaat?.

Usually I'm a good actor, but that day I was giving a high school play performance and the cop was about to throw some serious tomatoes. And by tomatoes I mean bullets.

COP: Can I see some passports and ID?

ME: So the thing is, we actually got lost on the freeway and then we ended up in Mexico. So we don't have passports.

COP: You ended up in Mexico?

ME: Ya. Funny, huh?!

Lisa and I started cracking up hysterically. But because of the tears and the incredible amount of fear pulsating through our veins, we looked like actual psychopaths having a nervous breakdown.

COP: Are you two ok?

I stopped laughing and went back to crying.

ME: I'm sorry. We're just really scared. Can you please help us?

COP: You know, driving through this lane is a federal offense. You know what happens to people who go through this lane without permission?

ME: They are really sorry?

COP: Oh ya. And they go to prison.

ME: Please don't send us to jail! We have children!

COP: You do?

ME: No. But we have a dog! And if we don't come home, she's gonna be so confused and probably shit EVERYWHERE!

COP: Pull your car over to the side and turn it off. I will deal with you two soon.

The cop walked away, and Lisa started hyperventilating. I pulled the car to the side of the road and turned it off like the cop told me to. I tried to calm down so I could be strong for Lisa.

ME: Everything is gonna be fine. He's just going to give us a warning and let us go home.

LISA: You think so?

ME: I know so.

And at that moment we saw the same cop make another car pull over to the side of the road in front of us.

ME: See, he's doing it to everyone. He probably just likes to scare people.

LISA: Ya, that's probably it.

Then I heard a bloodcurdling SCREAM and witnessed the cop RIP the driver out of the car and THROW him to the ground. The wife in the passenger seat jumped out of the car to save him while another cop ran over and TACKLED her to the ground like a football player from hell. Then four enormous bear-size dogs stampeded over and searched the entire car for drugs while cops handcuffed the couple and threw them into a cage!

LISA: Oh my God!!!
ME: Don't panic!

BUZZZZZ!!!! The cop Tasered the driver who was in the cage screaming in Spanish. The wife was crying and clawing at the cage until blood began dripping down her hands onto her arms. It was like the world was ending right in front of us.

LISA: Oh my God! We're gonna die!!!
ME: No! We're gonna be ok! Call your brother right now!

Lisa's brother spent years living in Mexico and knew a lot about the country. If anyone could help us figure out what to do, it was him. Lisa told him what happened and he started to laugh on the other line.

LISA: It's not funny! We are literally about to get thrown in a cage!
LISA'S BROTHER: No, you aren't. You guys are fine. They probably had drugs in their car.

Lisa looks over at me with a pissed look on her face. I mouth "I'm sorry" back at her.

LISA'S BROTHER: Listen, I've been through that line before. Just play
    dumb and act really scared and they will let you go with a warning.
LISA: Are you sure?
LISA'S BROTHER: Positive.

We both let out sighs of relief. I leaned over into my backseat
to double-check that there wasn't any weed anywhere. After feeling
around for a few seconds, I was relieved to find nothing except a
three-week-old, half-eaten Weight Watchers bar that luckily wasn't
illegal, just disgusting and kind of sad.

The cop walked back over to our window and leaned in with an
angry look on his face.

COP: What were you looking for in the backseat, boy?
ME: Nothing! Just my Weight Watchers bar!
COP: That looks old.
ME: Ya, I've been having a kind of cheat month. You know what I
    mean?
COP: No.
ME: Right. You're in shape. You don't need to diet. Look at those
    muscles! You're like the fuckin' Rock!

I go to touch his huge arm. He stops me.

COP: Don't touch me.
ME: Sorry.
COP: I'm going to let you go with a warning. But just know. Nothing
    would give me more pleasure than throwing your asses in prison
    right now. Especially you.

He took off his sunglasses and looked me up and down.

COP: I don't know what's wrong with you, but I feel really bad for her.

LISA: Thank you, Officer. I'll be ok.

COP: You sure? I can throw this idiot in jail and protect and serve you if you want.

Lisa blushed and chuckled.

LISA: Oh, Officer! You're too sweet.

ME: Wait, what?

COP: Alright, get the hell out of here before I change my mind.

As we headed back to Los Angeles, Lisa and I couldn't stop laughing. We were still in shock from the entire experience and could barely process what had happened. A few hours later we pulled into our driveway and turned off the car and sat in silence for a few minutes. It was all hitting us.

ME: Wow. That was insane.

LISA: Ya. Do you think that couple died?

ME: 100 percent.

LISA: Do you think that cop was serious about arresting you and hooking up with me?

ME: 110 percent.

LISA: You know I wouldn't have let him, right?

ME: Oh really? What would you have done?

LISA: I would have punched him in the face so he would have arrested me too. I'm not letting you go to jail alone.

ME: You know we would be in separate jails, right?

LISA: Nah, you could pass for a woman.

We laughed, and then I realized something.

ME: Hey, guess what.

LISA: What?

ME: We took a trip out of the country together.

LISA: Hey, I guess we did.

We gave each other a kiss and then sat in the car watching the sun go down. It might not have been the ideal vacation, but it definitely was unforgettable. Or as they say in Mexico, *inolvidable*. I had to Google that. You're welcome.

Too Many Melons:
The Story of Lauren Schnipper

About the Artist

WILLIAM KEECH began drawing at the age of two. For the past two decades he has continued to improve his work and has developed into an outstanding artist. His art and photography can be found on Instagram @wmkk92.

I can't begin to express my love for shitty reality TV. There's nothing I love more than coming home after a long day, curling up on the couch with a plate full of white-trash pizza nachos (chips covered in spaghetti sauce and Parmesan cheese), and watching four hours' worth of shows about people with lives worse than mine. It's much better than people watching in real life because if you scream, "WHAT A FUCKING LOSER!" at the mall, you'll most likely get kicked out. But at home you can scream at the screen all you want, and all you have to worry about is your neighbors thinking you're abusing your wife. It's what I like to call a dream Friday night. My DVR reads like a Wikipedia page for "a list of disgusting fucking things that will make you sick."

Shane's DVR

8:00 p.m.: THE WOMAN WITH 2 VAGINAS
8:30 p.m.: THE BOY WHO SHITS OUT OF HIS NECK
9:00 p.m.: TUMOR OR TWIN?
9:30 p.m.: THEY FOUND WHAAAAT INSIDE OF ME?

It's safe to say I have literally no taste. Anytime a friend recommends a show for me to binge and they start with "It's gonna get SO many Emmys," I tune out. I couldn't care less about a great plot with inspired performances. I'm looking for shows that dedicate entire budgets to providing the camera crew with barf bags and an on-set grief counselor. I want it BAD and I want it SAD.

One night as I was lying in bed covered in Dorito dust watching a show about teenage girls who are eight feet tall and pregnant I got a phone call from my agent.

ME: Hello?
AGENT: Shane! How's my superstar? Whatcha working on?? I bet you're SUPER busy!

I paused the pregnant giants.

ME: So busy. Literally elbow-deep in paperwork.

I licked my fingers and shoved my arm back inside the Dorito bag to get the last bit of crumbs.

AGENT: Well, I have something exciting to tell you!
ME: They're making *Josie and the Pussycats 2*, and they want me in it?!
AGENT: No. That movie was awful. You liked it?
ME: Of course not. I have better taste than that.

A DVR note popped up on my TV. "Are you still watching GIANT PREGNANT TEENS OF LA?"
I clicked YES.

AGENT: You got offered to be on a reality show!

It was at that moment my heart stopped. I don't know if it was because of my excitement or from the fact that I had just taken out a family-size bag of chips, but whatever it was caused me to yell at him in ALL CAPS.

ME: WHAT?! ARE YOU KIDDING ME?! WHICH ONE?! LIT-
    TLE PEOPLE OF LA? MY 600-POUND SAD LIFE? DO
    I GET TO SCOOP OUT DEAD CATS FROM A CRAZY
    WOMAN'S REFRIGERATOR?
AGENT: Good Lord. What the hell do you watch?
ME: Honestly, if you knew, you would drop me.
AGENT: This is a show about the making of your first movie! You
    will get to direct a film, and they will document the process! It's
    called *The Chair*.

I got to be on a reality show AND direct a movie? This was like finding out that the Take 5 bar had Reese's AND Crunch bars in it! Why was God SO good? The next day I told my mom the news, and she'd never been more proud of me.

ME: Mom! Guess what? I get to direct a movie!
MOM: That's great, honey!
ME: And it's part of a reality show!
MOM: JESUS CHRIST IS MY LORD AND SAVIOR, HALLELU-
    JAH!!!!!!

After I told my mom, it was time to talk to my producing part-ner Lauren. Lauren was my right-hand woman, and we worked on all my projects together. I had first met her in 2011 when I needed someone to help me with my first major short film. I interviewed her and knew right away we were a match made in heaven.

ME: So you seem to be really qualified. Do you have any questions for me?

LAUREN: Yes. How do you fit so many teeth in your mouth?

ME: What?

LAUREN: Your teeth. They're so big. Each one is, like, three teeth. I
can't stop staring at them.

HIRED. Anyone who had no filter and wasn't afraid to make fun
of my appearance was good with me. Lauren was in her early thirties,
and she was ready for a career change. She had tried her hand at acting, and she never made it. She had also tried stand-up comedy, but
she realized she was much better at sitting down. One time she gave
me a sampling of her old comedy routine. It reminded me of my
mom's upper lip after two weeks of not tweezing. ROUGH.

ME: Come on, tell me one of your old jokes!

LAUREN: Ok, this one used to KILL.

She got off my couch and stood in the middle of my living room
like she was on a comedy club stage. Unfortunately this all happened
before I started drinking, otherwise I would have gotten wasted.

LAUREN: Hey, what's the deal with those melon stands at the grocery
store? They stack those melons so high you can't reach 'em! Then
when you try to grab one from the middle, ALL the melons fall
off the stand! It's like, why can't I just get one melon and not fifty!

Crickets.

LAUREN: You're just not the demo, I guess.

My mom popped her head into the living room and started
cracking up.

MOM: That was HYSTERICAL! And it's SO TRUE!!!!!!

Lauren's face lit up with pride.

ME: Oh! I get it! You do mom humor!
LAUREN: Shut up! No I don't!
ME: You know what's even funnier?! You're doing mom humor and you don't even have kids!

Lauren looked at me with fire in her eyes.

MOM: You got any jokes about laundry??
LAUREN: Fuck my life.

For the next three years, working with Lauren on a daily basis was a blast . . . to the face with a cannon. And I mean that in the best way possible. She always kept me on my toes and always called me out on my shit. Not only was she there to help me create amazing content for my YouTube channel, she also was the only person in my life to tell me if I needed to do a juice cleanse to drop those five white-trash-nacho pounds. She did all the jobs I didn't want to do and all the jobs I didn't even know needed to be done. She acted as a casting director, a producer, a prop shopper, an art director, and sometimes a therapist when I needed it. Having her deal with all the mundane tasks of production allowed me to do what I do best: create. While she was doing the paperwork and negotiations, I was writing, editing, and coming up with fun video ideas. It was a great partnership. I trusted her with my entire being, and I imagined us working together forever. We would talk about making movies for the rest of our lives and running Hollywood together like a true power couple. She would be the man, of course.

Though we worked well together, we also had a lot of disagreements, but we always came out stronger afterward. Our fights were usually about things I'd force her to do that she felt were inappropriate.

LAUREN: No!

ME: Please! It's such a funny joke! The video is gonna be so good!

LAUREN: Shane, I can't ask a mother to let her five-year-old daughter snort Pixy Stix dust and pretend it's cocaine!

ME: Come on! Don't be a pussy!

LAUREN: Fine! But if it ruins some girl's life and makes her a drug addict when she grows up, I'm blaming you.

ME: If she watches my videos, her life is already fucked.

LAUREN: True.

After I found out about the reality-show opportunity, it was time to sit down with Lauren and see if it was something she wanted to be a part of. I could never make my first movie without her, so if she said no it was game over. I was really hoping she would say yes. I was also really hoping she would notice I'd lost two pounds from a pretty intense hot-sauce-and-lemon-juice-smoothie diet.

LAUREN: Do you really want to do a reality show? What if you look bad?

ME: What do you mean?

LAUREN: I know you think your jokes are funny, but sometimes they come off as mean, and what if they edit you to look like an asshole?

ME: You think my jokes are mean?

LAUREN: No, but I'm also an asshole. That's like shit asking throw up if it looks like crap.

ME: Am I the shit or the throw up?
LAUREN: Honestly? Both.
ME: Totes.

After talking more about it we decided we wanted to do it and we wanted to do it together. But her words forced me to consider what she was saying. I knew I had the tendency to get passionate when I worked. That passion could sometimes come across as anger. I was gonna try my best to keep it in check. The last thing I wanted to do was get into a fight with Lauren on camera and then have to watch it on television months later. Just the thought sounded awful. I have no idea how those pregnant giants watched their average-size boyfriends leave them for shorter girls over and over again. They repeat that show A LOT.

After Lauren and I agreed to be a part of the show it was time to move our lives to Pittsburgh for three months to work on our first full-length film, *Not Cool*. We lived in the same apartment building right next door to each other, which meant around midnight I would hear her FaceTiming with her husband and she would hear me asking Siri how close the nearest Cheesecake Factory was.

During the first few weeks of production we had a lot of fun and barely had any conflict. I think the only argument we had was over whether I should try wearing a fedora. I explained to her that fedoras are for really ugly people who need a distraction from their face. She explained to me that she owned three. It was a long night.

Naturally, being on a reality show was a lot different from what I had imagined because *The Chair* wasn't the kind of reality show I was used to watching. It was "highbrow" and "classy." YAWN. Bring on the weave snatching and the Jaws of Life opening up an obese lady's living room. They pretty much just documented our daily life and watched us make our first movie.

The only thing that felt reality showish was when my mom came to Pittsburgh to visit me, and the show producers asked to interview her. My mom came to the interview decked out in full hair, makeup, and jewels. She looked like a Real Housewife of YouTube (I'm gonna pitch that show btw. Look for it.), and she was ready to CRY. She sat down and the producer started asking her questions about me. She was anything but shy.

PRODUCER: So, Teresa, what is it like to watch your son live his dream?

After five minutes' crying happy tears she started to speak.

MOM: It's like watching a miracle happen right in front of my eyes.

She let out another epic cry, and the producer turned to me with the biggest smile I had ever seen. She was making reality-show gold.

PRODUCER: Thank you.
ME: Don't thank me, thank Bravo. They taught her well.

After my mom left, it was time to get back to work. That's when Lauren and I finally had our first big fight. Fortunately it happened off camera, so we wouldn't have to relive it months later when the show aired. I don't even remember what the fight was about, but I remember she cried and I didn't. I'm not a big crier when I'm having fights. I'm more of a sweater. If I leave a fight covered in man-boob sweat, you know it was a serious one. It's kind of ironic because fighting is one of the only times I don't cry. I cry at almost everything, including some TV commercials. I don't know what it is about commercials that make me tear up, but sometimes they hit me really hard. There was a cereal commercial a few years back that involved a kid sitting on his daddy's shoulders, and I just lost it. I'm not sure if I was jealous of the child's relationship with his father or if I was envious that he could ride an adult male's shoulders without giving him permanent spinal damage. The number of times I tried to ride someone's shoulders as a kid and was told "Sorry, I'm already at risk for scoliosis" were countless.

After the fight, Lauren and I made up and went out to eat. That was our usual pattern. We would scream and yell, she would cry, I would tell her she's not my mother, then we would go out to an Italian restaurant and order three bread baskets. Our fights were always long because we were both so stubborn. Sometimes we wouldn't even come to a conclusion. We would just get tired and super hungry, give up, and get pizza. It was our routine, and we were both used to it. Only later did I realize it was just me that was used to it. At the time, I had no idea the long-lasting effects it'd have on our relationship. But we'll get to that later.

During dinner we reminisced about the last few years and how far we'd come. The fact that we were making a movie was blowing our minds. What was even more mind-blowing was the fact that Lauren wasn't in an insane asylum for all the crazy shit I had made her do for me.

LAUREN: Do you remember the time you made me buy one thousand condoms from the 99 cent store for that video shoot?

ME: Oh ya. Just think, before you came along it was my mom who had to do all the prop shopping.

LAUREN: That explains your twisted relationship.

ME: Remember when you had to pick up that little-person actor from Hollywood Boulevard and bring him to my house?

LAUREN: You just HAD to write a video that called for a little person who looked like 50 Cent, didn't you?

ME: Hey, I had no idea he was going to make you pick him up.

LAUREN: When he got in my car he asked if he could pee in my empty coke bottle.

ME: Ya, I miss that little guy. Where do you think he is?

LAUREN: Literally dead.

ME: Probs.

The next two months of filming the movie were a blur. Then it was over. We had shot our first film, and it was amazing. I'd made so many awesome friends, and I had so many first experiences. First time directing a movie, first time in a starring role, first time living away from home, first time having a homeless person ask me if I was Jodie Foster (winter coats make me look very established), and last but not least, first time receiving confirmation that this was what I wanted to do for the rest of my life. I knew after that experience that I wanted to make movies forever and I wanted to make them with Lauren. Unfortunately the feeling wasn't mutual.

Those first few months back in LA were extremely hard on me. Not only did I break up with my longtime girlfriend, but I was dealing with a lot of personal issues. Being in Pittsburgh had felt like a vacation even though I was working, and once I came home, reality set in and it set in hard. Life wasn't a movie, it wasn't a reality show, it was a long, complicated stage play, and there's nothing I hate more than stage plays.

When *The Chair* finally aired, my whole life changed. Not because I became super famous or anything, but because I saw what everyone else did when they looked at me: a sometimes intense, dark guy with a lot of issues. On YouTube I can edit myself, and I can show the audience what I want them to see. On a reality-TV set, they are filming you all the time and you have no control over how you appear on-screen. Even though Lauren had warned me about this early on, I failed to consider it while we were filming because I was so focused on making my first movie. I wish I had thought about it more, because the number of double-chin angles that showed up in the final cut was horrifying.

One particular episode that was really hard to stomach was one in which Lauren and I got into a fight we didn't realize was being filmed. It was a fight I had forgotten about. A fight that wasn't unusual or out of the ordinary for us to have. But watching it made me sick.

The fight started because Lauren was rushing me through something because we were running out of time. Instead of understanding that she was just trying to help me accomplish everything I wanted to in the time allotted, I snapped at her and it turned into World War III. Granted she wasn't innocent either—there were probably much better ways for her to tell me to hurry up—but we were both in a high-stress environment. On the drive back to our apartment building in Pittsburgh she cried while she explained to me how much it hurt that I'd yelled at her in front of everyone. I felt like complete shit at the time, but it wasn't until I watched it unfold on TV that I didn't just feel like shit. I felt like shit AND throw up.

The next day Lauren came over to my house to have a talk with me. I assumed maybe she wanted to talk about the episode because I know I did. But what she had to say was something I didn't see coming.

LAUREN: I got a job offer.
ME: What?
LAUREN: There's a company that wants to hire me. And I think I want to take it.

In that moment our whole time working together flashed before my eyes. The good times, the bad times, the times we both tried the Paleo diet. All of it was flashing by, and I couldn't contain my tears. She wasn't just my producer, she was my best friend. And the thought of losing her was too much to put into words.

ME: But . . . why?

LAUREN: I love you, Shane. But I need to move on. I can't do it anymore. I want to have kids, go home at a decent hour every day. I really need a change.

ME: But I thought you wanted to make movies with me forever.

LAUREN: I did. But then we made one, and I realized it's not where my heart is. I don't want to live in a constant state of stress and worry about a million things at once. And all the fighting over the last few years has really worn me down.

ME: But I thought we were over that? We always get over it, don't we?

LAUREN: You get over it, Shane. It still affects me. I'm not twenty-something anymore. I'm tired. You know I love you so much. It's not just you. It's everything. But before I take this job I want to know your feelings.

My feelings were all over the place, but my main feeling was that I wanted her to be happy and that if this new job was what she needed to smile every day, then that's what I wanted for her.

ME: Take it.

Her face froze in shock. She started to tear up.

LAUREN: Really?

ME: Ya. I just want you to be happy.

I broke down in tears and she grabbed me for a hug.

LAUREN: I don't want you to hate me.
ME: I could never hate you. You're family to me.

After about thirty minutes of hugging and crying she left and I sat on my couch and let it all sink i n. Being on a reality show changed my life in more ways than I could have imagined. Not only did I finally see what I looked like from behind (not good), I saw how I treated the people I was closest to when I was stressed, and it was something I wanted to change. I never try to be mean, but when I'm in work mode I have a habit of letting my passion explode out of my body like fireworks out of a cardboard tube. Losing Lauren made me realize it was time to change and time to start to get a handle on my emotions.

To this day we are still friends, and who knows, maybe we will work together again at some point. But one thing is for sure, it won't be on a reality show, because between my double chin and her fedora, it's way too BAD and way too SAD for TV. Even for my DVR.

The Tale of
Big Lady Bertha

About the Artist

LAURA KEECH is a seventeen-year-old from Linden, Michigan, who has been practicing art all her life. She was born in Italy, lived in Moscow, Russia, for five years, then moved to the United States, where she began developing her talent. After Laura struggled for years to decide on a career to pursue, Shane's recognition of her drawings helped her to decide to pursue a career in art. You can follow her art page on Instagram @lauras_arts.

I've never been a car guy. When I was growing up I remember the men in my family all being obsessed with them. My dad would always have a beat-up car in the driveway with the hood lifted and rusty wires falling out all over the place. Sometimes I would try to act interested, but after about five minutes I would run out of car terms and just start babbling.

ME: Ya, Dad, that engine looks like the . . . faggeterator is broken.
DAD: Why are you out here?
ME: You're right. I'm gonna go inside and learn how to cross-stitch.
DAD: That makes more sense.

To this day when I'm buying a new car I don't have many preferences. My only requirement is that it's big enough to hold at least ten full Target bags but not big enough to help a friend move. That's my nightmare. I Uber to all my friends' houses because I'm terrified of them finding out I own a truck. The last thing I want is to spend a weekend helping one of my friends move their damp smelly mattress down a flight of stairs. I'd rather crochet a noose and hang myself with it.

When I was a kid I remember all the boys on my street would play with Hot Wheels and have races with each other. I was more interested in knives and stabbing them into the ground to see how it felt to kill somebody. I found that grass is the most satisfying. Lots of layers to get through and a nice RIPPING sound when you pull it out. I think that explains why I didn't have many friends.

Our first family car I remember getting remotely excited about was a truck that my dad purchased when I was around seven. It was near the end of my parents' marriage, and I'm pretty sure it was my dad's midlife crisis on wheels. It was a bright red pickup truck with a huge shell over the back. When you opened up the back there was carpeting, a couch, and even a mini fridge. At the time I thought it was the coolest thing ever. A little hangout inside of a truck! How cool is that? It's like a clubhouse on wheels! Now looking back, I realize he was probably planning his escape and wanted something mobile to live in. Wow.

Anyways, on my sixteenth birthday it was time for me to get my license and my first car. Hopefully something with a couch. At that age my mom was getting on my nerves, so it was a relief to consider a getaway plan.

It was eight in the morning and I had just woken up to the sound of my mom singing me a slightly altered version of the happy birthday song.

MOM: Happy birthday to Shaney. He's my little man-ey. He's now turning sixteen. I can't wait for him to have babies!

My mom had started pushing for grandkids the second I hit puberty. I'm not sure why she wanted smaller versions of me. The jumbo size seemed like enough. As I walked out to the kitchen, my mom was making pancakes shaped like the number sixteen. She wasn't the best cook, so they looked more like a cartoon wheelchair, but I wasn't picky. If it was edible, I'd eat it. Even if it wasn't edible, I would eat it. My favorite kind of pancakes are the ones that are drippy in the middle. I can't believe I have never had my stomach pumped. What a tiny miracle. As I scarfed down my edible handicapped parking sign, my mom sat down and helped me prep for my driving test that I was going to be taking that day.

MOM: Ok, what do you do if a streetlight goes out while you are driving up to it?

ME: Freak out and wonder if the rapture is coming?

MOM: No, that's only if ALL the streetlights go out.

ME: Right.

MOM: You just treat the intersection as a four-way stop sign.

ME: What if there's no one around? Can I just go through it?

MOM: Do the calories in a pack of Oreos still count if it's midnight and no one sees you eat it?

Damn it. From experience I knew they did. I was terrified of this driving test. I was a pretty good student in school, but for some reason the driving classes were really challenging for me. It might have been because I had an insane instructor. I remember on that first day of class, when he gave me our assignment for the day, I knew it wasn't going to work out.

INSTRUCTOR: Ok, so today you are going to drive me to Big Lots 'cause they got a sale on plates and cups, and then you are gonna drive me to my ex-girlfriend Rhonda's house to pick up my last box of shit from her place. If I'm in there for longer than five minutes, assume some shit went down and start the car so we can get out fast. Got it?

ME: Where do I get a bus pass?

It was time for my driving test, and my mom and I pulled into the DMV parking lot while a Kelly Clarkson anthem blared from our CD player. No song was more perfect for this moment than "Breakaway." I truly was going to spread my wings and learn how to fly. Hopefully I wouldn't fly into oncoming traffic and kill me and my instructor. Although if I worked at the DMV, I might have wanted someone to fly me into traffic. I got up to the front desk and they assigned me to my person. She looked nice and nonthreatening, so I was excited. This was going to be a piece of cake! And then she opened her mouth.

DMV WORKER: You got air-conditioning? My pits are dripping more than a turkey in a rotisserie cooker.

As delicious as that metaphor sounded, I had a feeling she was going to be a nightmare. We got into my car and she pulled out her wallet. She opened it up, and there was a picture of her and three children.

DMV WORKER: You see them? Those are my kids. My life is in your hands today. If you crash and take me into the fiery beyond, you aren't just disappointing your family. You are destroying these children's lives and leaving them in the custody of their piece of shit father who doesn't even know their names. He calls one of them Eggplant 'cause he says that's what her head looks like.

I looked at the picture, and I knew exactly which girl he called Eggplant. Why would God do that to a child? Heartbreaking. We started the test and at first it was going pretty well. I actually wasn't as nervous as I thought I would be. I made all the correct turns, did all the right motions, and even stopped for a cat that was running across the street. Lucky for me, my instructor was for sure a cat lady, so that got me some extra points. As we pulled back into the DMV parking lot she looked at me with the picture of her family in her hand.

DMV WORKER: They thank you for not killing their momma.

I looked at the picture of frowning vegetable-shaped children and gave it a thumbs-up. She handed me my test results, and I passed with flying colors. It was time for me to hit the road and take over the world, or at least take over the nearest drive-thru for some celebratory milk shakes.

The next day it was time for me to pick out my first car. I had saved up for a while, and my mom was going to help me with the down payment. We didn't really have enough for anything fancy, but I was ok with that. I'm not a fancy guy. As long as there was a way to play Kelly Clarkson as loud as humanly possible I would be satisfied. We went to a used-car lot and scoped out our choices. Most of the cars looked like they had been stepped on by the foot of God, but there was one car that looked almost decent. It was a beige deep-fried-colored four-door Chevy Malibu with only three dents in the hood instead of twelve, like the other options.

MOM: You know what that looks like?
ME: A big chicken nugget with a few nibbles in the hood.

She looked it over again.

MOM: Yes. Yes, it does. Interesting. But what I was going to say was . . . a WINNER!

I agreed, and we gave each other a victory hug. My first car and it was all mine! Well, technically it was also my mom's, since she helped me pay for it. And it was also anyone's who had owned it before me and left their numerous stains in the backseat, but either way, I was excited. That afternoon after we left the dealership it was time for me to take my first ride with it alone. I got inside the car and just looked around for a few minutes. I soaked it all in and couldn't believe I had my own car. It felt like just yesterday I had played with Hot Wheels, pretending there was a little me inside driving. Wait, that wasn't my life. That was a normal boy's. I had crocheted sweaters for our chinchilla.

As I sat in my new ride I decided it was time to give it a gender and a name. I have a thing about naming inanimate objects. My bed at the time was named Nana, because lying on it was like snuggling into a big old-lady hug. My TV's name was Freddie Prinze Jr. because it rarely worked. I even named my toilet Dr. Phil, because it was full of shit. So naming my car was a big deal, and it had a lot to live up to. I pressed my palms against the dashboard and tried to feel its personality. The car was definitely a she. The second I entered her I knew that she had a feminine vibe. There was a softness to her but also a bitchiness that I liked. Her seats were comfortable but every once in a while a spring would pop up and stab me in the ass. I liked her sassiness. She was also large and in charge and wasn't afraid to speak her truth. She was pretty loud with her squeaky breaks and old engine, so you always knew when she was coming. I started speaking to her to see if a name might just pop out.

ME: Hey, beautiful. How are you feeling? Do you feel good? Are you ready to hit the town and make all the boys stare?

Her engine purred like a kitten and vibrated my entire body.

ME: How old are you? Are you an angsty teenager? Or are you a wise, older woman?

She made a humming sound as her engine started to settle. She seemed relaxed. Comfortable. Ready to explore. As I looked around the interior I noticed all the tears and rips. She had gone through so much. She wasn't a young un'; she was older and wise. Fender benders, family fights, drunken mistakes, and from one stain that caught my eye a possible child birth. This wasn't any average woman. This was an elder. The name hit me, and I knew it was perfect for her.

ME: I'm going to call you Big Lady Bertha.

POP POP POP. Her engine let out a noise of excitement. I could tell she agreed with the name choice. It was time for Shane and Bertha to begin their new life together.

That night I called my friends and told them the news that I had gotten a car, so we decided to all go out and have the time of our lives. I picked up my friends Tara, Kelley, and Katy for the first time. I felt like a pimp picking up my ladies. Except none of them wanted to have sex with me, and there's no way a pimp would ever drive a car with a cupcake freshener dangling from the rearview mirror. As they climbed in, they looked around the car and freaked out.

KATY: This car is awesome! It smells like it's lived such an interesting life.
KELLEY: Ya, someone definitely died in here. But I don't get a violent vibe.
TARA: I love the fabric on the ceiling! It would feel so good if you were lying back here with your hands and feet up against it while some guy you met at Dave and Buster's drilled you into the seat.
ME: You are aware that's your life, not mine, right?
TARA: Ya, which reminds me. Can I borrow your car sometime?
ME: Definitely not. There are enough stains back there as it is.
KATY: So what should we do? See a movie? Go get fro yo? Drive to the beach?

KELLEY: Ooooh! We could drive to the cemetery and have a picnic on
    my grandpa!
TARA: Kelley, we're never going to do that. Stop asking every weekend.
ME: I have a better idea.

I had never been a risk taker. I always did the right thing, and I
never broke any rules in school. Even when the kids in my class were
experimenting with alcohol or pot, I was experimenting with different mix-ins at Cold Stone's. But there was one thing I had always
wanted to do that I had seen in every teen movie as a kid.

ME: Let's egg someone's house!

My friends were shocked that I wanted to do something illegal
but were all very much in for it. The craziest thing we had ever done
on a Friday night was prank call my mom and tell her I had a heart
attack. It's sad how many times she believed it. When we got to the
store, we walked down the aisles looking for our weapon of choice.

KATY: There's the eggs! How many should we get?
ME: Wait . . . I have a better idea.

My eyes began to wander around the condiment section. I
grabbed a few bottles of ketchup and ranch dressing.

TARA: We're gonna make Thousand Island?
ME: No. What if we drive by people's cars on the street and squirt
    ketchup and ranch at them?!

They all looked at me confused. I had seen a show on TV years before that showed kids driving around their neighborhood, and every time

they passed a car on the street they would spray ketchup at it. It looked so funny and also pretty safe, considering we could just drive away as fast as we could. When you egg someone's house, there's a risk of them walking outside and catching you midthrow. When you are spraying condiments, you are already driving. It's the perfect getaway. I'm not sure why it sounded like a good idea at the time, but I was dead set on it.

ME: Come on, guys, lets go KETCHUPING!

Even though my friends were confused, they were all on board. We filled up our cart with condiments and we were on our way! As we drove into the first neighborhood I opened up a bottle of ketchup, and Tara opened up a bottle of ranch. We unrolled the windows and scoped out our targets.

ME: Ok, what about that car. It looks super douchey. I bet whoever owns it is a total asshole.
TARA: He is. I hooked up with him last year during the fire drill. Afterward he told me he only hooked up with me because he didn't know it was a drill and he thought he was gonna die.
KELLEY: Wow, you sure know how to pick 'em.
ME: Alright, everybody, get your bottles ready!

We stuck our bottles out the window.

ME: On the count of three! One, two, three!

SQUIRRRRRRT! We all squeezed the bottles to the breaking point and completely covered the douche mobile in layers of thick sugary sludge. I peeled out and drove away as fast as I could. We were all laughing like maniacs.

TARA: I can't believe we did that!!!!

KATY: I feel like we just KILLED somebody!!!

KELLEY: Me too! It feels even better than I imagined!

ME: Let's do it again!!!

And for the next three hours we went through about fifteen bottles of ketchup and ranch dressing and destroyed more than twenty cars. We firmly believed we were criminal masterminds. We were down to our last few bottles, so we had to make sure it was good. Our final mission!

ME: Guys, we should ketchup a teacher's car.

The girls all screamed with excitement. We were drunk with power, and we were ready to devour another victim. As we pulled up to one of our teacher's houses we noticed that someone was on the porch.

KATY: I think I see someone sitting out front.

KELLEY: Maybe it's just a shadow.

KATY: A shadow shaped exactly like a human?

KELLEY: You would be surprised what form shadows can take in the darkness when they want to fool the living.

KATY: How are we friends? Seriously, how did that happen?

TARA: Guys, maybe we shouldn't ketchup this one. What if they call the cops?

ME: Come on! Don't chicken out on me now! This is our last time! Let's make it special.

TARA: I've heard that one before and it definitely ended with cops being called.

ME: Trust me, we'll be fine. Let's do this!

We all unrolled our windows and stuck the bottles out, ready to squeeze.

ME: Ok, on the count of three! One, two, three!

SQUEEEEEEEEZE! The car parked in front of the house got covered in condiments. But then a figure popped up out of nowhere. We didn't have time to stop, which meant our teacher's husband got SQUIRTED with ketchup and ranch. I could see his shocked red-and-white-covered face as we sped away.

TARA: Oh my God!!!! We hit a person!!
KATY: DRIVE!!!!!

I peeled out as fast as I could and the girls were screaming in the backseat like we had just fled a drive-by shooting.

ME: Everyone, calm down! It's gonna be ok!

A cop siren blared behind us.

TARA: This is just how it happened last time!

I could hear the sirens, but I couldn't see any flashing lights. Maybe they weren't trying to find me? Maybe it was a coincidence? Just when I convinced myself everything was fine, a cop peeled around the corner and was coming right for us! Instead of pulling over, I decided to book it and get the hell out of there. I didn't want to get pulled over on my first day of driving, and I definitely didn't want my mom to find out that I had gone around town throwing ketchup at strangers' cars. She would probably have thrown me in rehab just as a precaution! Finally the cop car was far enough behind us that I didn't think he saw my taillights, so I turned a few corners and ended up in the middle of a dark road near a park.

ME: I think I lost him.
KELLEY: Did we just seriously flee a scene and drive away from the cops?
ME: Yes, we did.
KELLEY: Cool!!

We all started laughing hysterically, mostly out of fear and built-up adrenaline. I started my car back up again and decided it was time to end the night.

ME: Guys, I think we should find a Dumpster and get rid of all this evidence.

As I pulled Bertha away from the curb, we heard a loud THUD.

KATY: What was that?
TARA: It sounded like you hit something.
ME: I'm sure it's fine.

Then we heard a loud SCREAM coming from underneath the car.

KELLEY: You guys heard that, right? Or was that just in my head again?

Then we heard a scratching sound and when I turned to my left I saw a small figure crawling out from underneath my car and running into the wilderness.

ME: I think I hit a possum or something. But it seems to be ok.

TARA: Wait . . . Do you guys smell that?

And in a matter of seconds a smell filled my car that was so intense, so wretched, so absolutely awful that we all started to scream and gag.

ME: Skunk!!!

We all rushed out of the car and started coughing up our lungs. The smell was so bad that Katy started vomiting.

KATY: I can't stop throwing up!!!!

As I watched her hurl her guts out on the side of a tree I couldn't help but realize how much it looked like she was "ketchuping" that tree. Then it hit me. This was karma. This was God's punishment for what we had done that night. And we deserved it. I checked the inside of the car to see if the smell was gone but it had only gotten worse! It was as if the skunk had left his ass inside the engine.

KELLEY: What should we do? Should we call someone?
ME: No! I don't want my mom to know about this. Let's just drive it around for a while and hopefully the smell will wear off. We can go to the store and get some Febreze!
TARA: Um, I'm pretty sure Febreze doesn't make a scent that can cover rotting asshole. Trust me, I've looked.
ME: Please, guys! Let's just roll down the windows and try to air it out.

We got inside the car and rolled down the windows. We all breathed through our mouths and kept our noses shut as tightly as we could. I drove for about ten feet when Katy started vomiting again. This time ALL OVER BERTHA.

KATY: I'm sorry! I accidentally sniffed!

She ran out of the car and continued spraying puke all over the place like one of those wacky sprinkler noodles kids play with in the summer. Except a lot less fun and a lot more chunks. I grabbed my phone and decided it was time to tell the truth and call my mom. I was so scared she was going to be upset and force me to live in my skunk-infested car, but instead when I told her she couldn't stop laughing.

MOM: You hit a skunk?!
ME: It's not funny! The smell is making Katy barf up blood! I think she actually might be dead.

Katy was laying on the side of the road twitching like roadkill.

MOM: Alright, I'll come pick you guys up. Call the tow truck company and let's have that car looked at in the morning.
ME: Thanks, Mom. I'm sorry.
MOM: Just know that what goes around comes around. And when you threw ketchup on those people's cars, it was all gonna come back to you in some way.

She was right. Karma was a bitch. But I didn't know how much of a bitch until the next day when the mechanic told me that the smell in my car would be there for six months and that there was no way to clean it out.

ME: WHAT?!

MECHANIC: Sorry, man. Skunk smell is powerful stuff. You got to just drive it around and air it out. You might need another one of these cupcake fresheners . . . or a hundred.

So for the next six months, anytime I stopped at an intersection the drivers in the cars around me would start gagging and roll up their windows. My friends refused to ride in my car because it would make them nauseous. The only reason I was ok was because I got used to it. My clothes, my hair, my entire being smelled like rotting asshole, and there was nothing I could do about it. All because I thought it would be a fun idea to throw ketchup and ranch at strangers' cars. Poor Bertha didn't deserve it. I failed her. But I learned my lesson and I never did anything that stupid again.

A couple of years later I traded in Bertha for another car and I have no idea where she is now. Every time I pass a busted-looking car that looks like a chicken nugget I think of her and wonder if she misses me. And every time I smell something so foul that it makes me want to gag it reminds me of how much I don't miss her.

• • •

Good-bye, Big Lady Bertha.

The Ghost of My Grandma

About the Artist

TIN HOANG is an eighteen-year-old photographer based in a small town in Sweden. He discovered his passion for art at an early age, but later discovered the power of photography alongside fashion. Tin always pushes the boundaries and is using his photography to tell a story in an artistic, stylish, aggressive, and bold way, which makes him one unique young photographer to keep an eye on. Follow him on Instagram @TINHOANGS and see his online portfolio at tinhoangs.com.

Photograph by Thein Hoang Photography.

The year: 2011. The time: twelve thirty a.m. The mood in my bedroom: What the fuck am I doing with my life and why is there a box full of wigs sitting on my dresser? It was a typical Monday night, and I was sitting up in bed, flipping through channels on my TV that was so big it was embarrassing. You know those TVs that you see in people's houses and you can't help but yell DOUCHE when you see them? Ya, it was one of those.

As I flipped past rerun after rerun of some nineties sitcoms I heard a noise coming from my closet. The house I was living in at the time was pretty old, so I never got scared of the creaks that came from inside the walls. I just assumed the house was falling apart and there were probably rats crawling around behind the drywall. Nothing to be scared of. You can take the boy out of the projects, but you can't take the projects out of the boy! But when I set my remote down on my bedside table, I noticed something move inside the closet. The hair on the back of my neck stood up, and I felt a chill go down my spine. I froze and started breathing heavily. I couldn't move, and the room started to feel like it was closing in on me. I felt a pressure on my chest as if something was pushing into me with all the force it could muster. The figure began moving slowly. I knew it couldn't be my cat or a breeze blowing through, so I built up the courage to slowly move my eyes toward my closet, and as I did I could feel energy building. I finally focused my eyes directly on the closet, and my heart stopped.

Standing in front of me was my grandmother. She was wearing her signature purple robe and had a look of worry on her face. Pretty typical for Grandma. There was just one problem. My grandmother was dead.

This was the first time I had ever seen a ghost. I'd had experienced many paranormal moments in my life, but none of them had ever been this real or this close-up. My grandma had died two years earlier, and I had felt her presence around me ever since. I was still having dreams at least twice a week in which she would come to me and just hang out like old times. We would watch TV, walk around the grocery store and talk about how expensive everything was, and of course try on each other's clothes. I had a thing for big nightshirts and she had a thing for, well, big nightshirts. And considering my shirts were extra huge, they were perfect for her naps. I always wished that one day I would see her again in real life. The second I actually did and she was standing in my closet glaring at me, I changed my mind. It was horrifying.

I sat and stared at her for a few moments and wasn't able to move. I couldn't scream, couldn't breathe, couldn't look away. It was as if I was in some trance and she had a hold over me. As she started to open her mouth to speak, I finally built up the nerve to get out of my bed and run out the door. As I ran into the hallway I started screaming for my brother and my mom.

ME: MOM! JERID!!

They rushed into the hallway to see what was going on. I fell to the floor, nauseous. I was in shock and I couldn't quite process what the hell had just happened to me.

MOM: What's going on??
JERID: Dude, are you ok?
ME: I saw . . . I saw . . .

As I tried to explain, my brother cut me off.

JERID: Grandma?

ME: How did you know?

JERID: 'Cause I heard her voice right before you started screaming.

MOM: I felt something too. I could smell her perfume in my room.

We all stood in the hallway feeling really confused but also really comforted by each other. If they hadn't believed me, I don't know what I would have done. There's nothing worse than people telling you you're crazy.

JERID: Let's go look.

We all turned our heads toward my bedroom door and started walking slowly over to it. My mom grabbed our hands and started whispering prayers. With each step closer, I started feeling the hairs on my neck rising again. It was like a static-covered balloon was being lowered onto my back. As we opened the door we turned the corner and looked in the closet. No one was there.

ME: She's gone.

JERID: Wait, was she right here?

Jerid walked over to the closet and pointed at a particular area.

ME: Ya. Standing right there.

Jerid grabbed something that had been hanging right where she had been standing. He pulled it out. It was my grandma's signature purple robe.

JERID: Dude. She was standing in front of her robe.

Every hair on my body stood up and every square inch of my skin was covered with goose bumps. When my grandma died each member of the family went through her belongings and picked out things that were special to them. Most everyone took stuff that was worth money because before my grandma died she'd said—

GRANDMA ON DEATHBED: Take whatever crap you want and sell it on eBay. I don't care. Shane, make sure to eat the leftover pie in my fridge. I don't want it to go bad.

What a caring woman. Instead of taking something I could pawn for cash, I decided to take the robe that I had seen her wear every day I'd known her. It was as if her job in life had been to make me fat and happy, and that robe was her uniform. I didn't want it to go into the trash or to Goodwill, so I decided to stow it away in my closet. The pie, on the other hand, was gone the second I laid eyes on it. Damn, that woman knew how to pick out a good pie. It was peanut butter and banana in memory of her crush, Elvis. Her Elvis shirts were the only big sleep shirts of hers I didn't touch. I was scared of what she did in them.

JERID: Dude. Do you think she wanted to tell you something?
ME: I don't know. She looked worried. But that might be because she saw me jerking off to *Cupcake Wars*.
MOM: What?
ME: Sorry, forgot you were here.

The next day I walked down to the kitchen and my mom was sitting at the counter looking at old pictures of us with Grandma. She was crying as she flipped through an old, tattered photo album.

MOM: You guys really had a strong connection. She sure loved you.

ME: Ya, I think it's 'cause we both hated everything.

MOM: Well, you definitely didn't hate each other.

ME: Only sometimes. Mainly when she would ask me to try on bras at Macy's so she could see what they looked like on.

MOM: I miss her so much.

I missed her too. I thought about her every time I passed the bra section in a department store. I also thought about my sexuality and questioned a lot of things, but that's a different story. My mom had a hard time dealing with my grandma's death. My mom kept a kind of shrine dedicated to her in her bedroom. Her dresser was full of framed pictures of her mother, and there were little knickknacks from my grandma's old apartment scattered around. Walking into Mom's room was kind of like walking into a museum of my grandma. I knew it wasn't healthy, but who was I to tell her how to grieve. I literally ate an entire sheet cake when I found out *Sister, Sister* had been canceled. They didn't even give it a finale episode! Heartless assholes.

The next day I was talking to a friend about what happened and they suggested I hire some ghost hunters to come to my house to investigate. Part of me felt weird about it and thought it was disrespectful to the dead. The other part of me thought it would be good vlogging material for my YouTube channel, so I found a ghost hunter as soon as I could!

I invited my friend Steve to come over the night the ghost hunters came to my house. I thought it might make for some good entertainment and he loved paranormal stuff. But truth be told, I was terrified that a random dude who thought he could talk to dead people would be inside my house, so I wanted to fill it with as many witnesses as possible. When the ghost hunter arrived, he gave us a rundown of how the night was going to go.

GHOST HUNTER: Alright! Here's how it's gonna go down. We are gonna set up night-vision cameras all around your house and set sensor alarms around every area that we deem a portal.

ME: What's a portal?

GHOST HUNTER: A location that the ghosts use to come here from the other side.

ME: Makes sense.

GHOST HUNTER: We also are going to use this heat sensor device to tell us when a spirit is in our presence.

JERID: What about a Ouija board?

GHOST HUNTER: You better be fucking kidding. Do you want to die tonight, son?

JERID: No.

GHOST HUNTER: Good. Then stick with me and don't try anything stupid.

JERID: Come on, bro, isn't this whole thing kind of stupid?

The Ghost Hunter got in Jerid's face with the glare of a pro wrestler about to take down a competitor.

GHOST HUNTER: You think this is funny, bro? You know what's not funny? A demon coming through a portal disguising itself as your grandma and possessing your mother so that she kills herself.

MOM: Wait, WHAT?!

GHOST HUNTER: Sorry, forgot you were here.

Twelve thirty a.m. rolled around. The time that I had seen my grandma in my closet. The Ghost Hunter made his way through my house with his detectors and other shit I didn't understand. My friends and I walked slowly behind him, ready to be traumatized. As we walked past my mom's room his detector started going crazy.

GHOST HUNTER: Wait . . . there's something in this room.

MOM: That's my room.

GHOST HUNTER: Not anymore.

He slowly opened the door, and we all took a deep breath. As he stepped over the threshold, his detector beeped louder.

GHOST HUNTER: It's really strong in here. Did your grandma ever spend time in this room?

ME: No. She died before we bought this house.

GHOST HUNTER: Well, she must be making up for lost time, because she is definitely here.

His detector started to go insane as he walked by the closet.

GHOST HUNTER: She's in here.

STEVE: Wow, Shane, she's in the closet! You guys really do have a lot in common.

ME: Very funny.

STEVE: Meh. Not my best.

The ghost hunter opened the closet and put his detector inside. BEEP BEEP BEEP!!! The detector started to burn his hand.

GHOST HUNTER: Ow! It's making this thing so hot. This is really intense. She really wants us to know she's with us.

All the lights were out, so it was hard to see. As the ghost hunter reached deeper into the closet, his detector hit an object and broke.

GHOST HUNTER: Wow. I've never had this happen before. What's back here?

MOM: Um, I don't know. Just random things. Clothes. Pictures . . . oh wait.

My mom's face went white. She remembered what was in the closet. She walked over and reached in. As she did, we all started to smell something familiar.

JERID: What is that?
STEVE: It smells like perfume.
ME: It's hers.

My mom pulled out the object that had broken the detector. I shined my flashlight on it and we saw that it was a large picture of my grandmother. We all gasped, and my mom dropped the picture in shock.

GHOST HUNTER: She's here.

We all got really quiet. None of us knew what to say. None of us wanted to speak because we were afraid we would start a conversation with the dead. Then my mom started crying and picked up the picture.

MOM: Momma. It's me. Are you here?

As a tear fell from her cheek I could see the hope in her eyes. She wanted to talk to her mother so badly. Things had just gotten very real for all of us.

GHOST HUNTER: Ethel, if you are here with us, gives us a knock on the wall.

After a moment of silence a soft knock was heard in the room. We all held our breaths. My mom continued.

MOM: Mom. I miss you so much.
ME: I miss you too, Grandma.
JERID: Me too.
STEVE: We all do.

Everyone in the room started to get emotional. We could all feel her presence and we could all feel that she wanted to communicate so badly but couldn't. Then we heard another knock.

GHOST HUNTER: Ethel, if you are having trouble crossing over to the other side give us a knock. We can help you.

Silence. No knock.

GHOST HUNTER: If she isn't having trouble crossing over then that means she came here to tell you something or to help you in some way.
ME: Grandma. Is there something you want to tell me?

Knock.

ME: What is it?

Knock.

GHOST HUNTER: She can't speak the way we do. You might need to see a medium.
ME: But I thought that's what you did?

GHOST HUNTER: I only find the ghosts and help them back to the light. You need someone to translate.

So the next day I began my search for a medium. Never in my life did I think I would need to find someone to help me talk to a dead person. How do you even find that? Luckily one of my friends had a family friend who was a legit medium. She had solved murders and predicted historical events. I knew if I wanted to talk to my grandma, I would have to see her.

I walked up to the medium's front door with sweaty palms and a lump in my throat. I didn't know what to expect. Was my grandma going to show herself again? Was she going to tell me something I didn't want to hear? Was she going to ask why I touched myself to Food Network competition shows? So many questions were running through my mind, and all I wanted to do was find out the answers. The door opened and standing in front of me was a sweet-looking woman with kind eyes. There was a shaggy golden retriever at her feet, so I instantly trusted her.

MEDIUM: You must be Shane.
ME: Yes. Thank you so much for meeting with me.
MEDIUM: Wow. You have so many spirits around you.
ME: Really? That would explain all the voices in my head!

I laughed. She didn't.

MEDIUM: Yes, it would. Don't listen to them. Some aren't on your side.

Fuck.

MEDIUM: Come in.

She guided me down the stairs into a basement that had been converted into her reading room. It felt safe and calm, so I wasn't as scared as I should have been walking down into a stranger's basement. I sat down on the couch facing her and she instantly knew what I had come for.

MEDIUM: You're here to talk to your grandmother, aren't you?

I hadn't told her that on the phone. She only knew that ghosts were trying to contact me.

ME: Yes. Wow. How did you know?
MEDIUM: She's here with you. Sitting right next to you.

At that point I'm pretty sure I shat myself. I felt my grandma's energy, but I was too scared to look over my shoulder.

MEDIUM: Wow. She sure loves you. She's looking at you and she can't stop smiling.

I started to tear up.

ME: Ya. She was my rock.
MEDIUM: You guys were very similar. Almost like soul mates.
ME: She was my best friend.

The medium smiled. I felt calm. I wasn't scared anymore. The energy from my grandma was all love. I wasn't afraid like I had been that night in my bedroom. It was different now.

ME: What does she look like? I heard that when you die you go back to your young self.

MEDIUM: Yes, that's true. You go back to the age you were when you felt the best about yourself. She looks to be in her thirties. Beautiful black hair. A pastel-colored dress. Sparkling blue eyes. What a gorgeous woman.

ME: Really? When I saw her in my closet she was older and wearing a robe.

MEDIUM: She wanted to look familiar to you. How you remembered her. If she had come to you like this you wouldn't have known who it was.

ME: Ya, I probably would have thought there was a dead hooker in my room.

MEDIUM: Hey! You made her laugh!

ME: She and I share a sick sense of humor.

MEDIUM: I can see that. I also feel a negative energy. She was kind of a . . .

ME: Bitch?

MEDIUM: I didn't say it, you did.

ME: She and I had a shared view on life. Pretty much *fuck everything*.

MEDIUM: Well, she still has that for sure. Sorry, Ethel.

ME: So what does she want to tell me?

The medium directed her attention just to my right.

MEDIUM: Ethel, what would you like your sweet grandson to know? What are you trying to tell him?

After a few moments of silence the medium got her answer. She turned back to me with a look of concern.

MEDIUM: She's worried about you. She says you have too many things going on in your business life and you are slowly burning out.

She says you are spinning too many plates and that if you don't give yourself a break, you are going to wear yourself down.

ME: I do have a lot going on. But I like to work.

MEDIUM: There's a difference between liking to work and using work as a way to avoid your problems. She says that you have some personal issues you need to deal with and that you need to let go of some of the work so you have time to deal with them. She's scared for you, Shane. She says she can feel your energy dying.

She was right. I hadn't taken a day off in five years. I was so consumed with my work that I had let everything else in my life fall by the wayside. I didn't have time for healthy relationships, I didn't give myself time to recharge, and I definitely wasn't taking care of my health. I was slowly fading away, and everyone in my life had started to notice. I suppose I was just in denial.

MEDIUM: She loves you so much and she wants you to be happy. She says that the only way to find happiness is to be open to it. Stop hating yourself so much. That is her one regret. She feels that she passed her hatefulness on to you.

ME: But that's where my humor comes from. I'm so blessed to have inherited that part of her.

MEDIUM: Yes, but she wants you to let some of the hatefulness go so you can enjoy life more. Something she didn't get to do.

I felt a touch on my hand. My arm hair stood up once again and a chill spread throughout my body.

MEDIUM: You feel that, don't you?

ME: Yes. What is it?

MEDIUM: She's holding your hand. She's with you, Shane. Always. She wants you to know that.

I wiped a tear from my eye and let out a sigh. I felt safe. Loved. It was an amazing feeling.

MEDIUM: She also wants to tell your mother something.

ME: What?

MEDIUM: She wants to tell your mother to let go of her. She says that there is some kind of shrine in your mother's room? Memorabilia from your grandma's life? Does that sound familiar?

ME: Yes. Mom keeps all her stuff on the dresser and looks at it every day.

MEDIUM: Your grandma wants her to pack that stuff up so she can move on. She's been trying to tell her for weeks. It's not healthy to be stuck in the past. She needs to heal.

I knew that my mom needed to pack up all that stuff, but I hadn't had the heart to tell her. But maybe if Grandma wanted her to, she would do it. After I left the medium, I went home to talk to my mom. I was concerned at first when I didn't see her in the living room watching Bravo like she usually did every night at eight.

ME: Mom?

I heard her shout from her bedroom.

MOM: I'm in here, sweetie!

I walked into her bedroom and saw a box on her bed filled with my grandma's knickknacks. She was packing up all the stuff on her dresser.

ME: What are you doing?

MOM: Something told me it was time to let go. I think I'm ready to move on. I love her so much, but I have to get over it. It's just so hard.

ME: Ok, this is so crazy because I was just at the medium's house, and she told me that Grandma wanted you to pack up your shrine to her. She said she has been trying to tell you for weeks.

My mom's eyes filled with tears. My grandma had finally made the connection and told my mom it was ok to move on. It was a truly beautiful moment. My mom was so overwhelmed she moved to the bed and sat down. I walked over to her and sat down next to her. I grabbed her for a hug and we just held each other while we cried. It wasn't a sad cry; it was a happy cry. My grandma cared so much for us and wasn't going to stop haunting us until she got us to listen to her. Most ghosts need help moving on. This time it was us who needed the help. And I'm so glad my stubborn, crazy, awesome grandma was there to guide us.

I love you, Grandma. Now stop haunting me and go fuck Elvis. I know you've always wanted to. Get it, girl. Get it.

Human Trash

About the Artist

STEVEN PAANANEN, a self-inflated, full-time balloon artist from Boston, Massachusetts, started twisting balloons when he was sixteen. Now, at the age of twenty-three, he spends his weekends twisting at kids' parties by day, then at karaoke bars by night. In his free time, he entertains people by creating zany Snapchat stories with his balloon art. Become his friend on Snapchat and Instagram @StevenBalloons.

"*Not Cool* by YouTube Star Shane Dawson is a waste of time . . . comedy that only date-rapists, racists, and socio-paths could love."

—*Los Angeles Times*

"No one involved (with *Not Cool*) should ever be allowed to work in the movies again."

—*The New York Times*

This wasn't the first time I'd gotten a bad review. My entire You-Tube career had been a one-sided game of darts. I put myself out there, and millions of people had the power to throw their criticisms my way and see how many will affect me. But this didn't just start when I decided to create a YouTube channel. I'd been getting slammed by reviews like this since I was in high school.

The first painful attack on my comedic style came from my psychology teacher, Mr. Roberts, when I was in my junior year of high school. What he said about me makes the *Los Angeles Times* look like My Little Pony.

It was the first day of psychology class, and I was excited to learn about how my brain worked. I knew that for the most part it was powered by Diet Coke and Sharpie sniffs, but I wanted to know the real inner workings of my mind. Why did I have an obsession with dogs? Why is it so hard for me to focus on one thing at a time?

Why are there so many members of the Black Eyed Peas when only will.i.am speaks? So many questions.

As I walked into the classroom, I noticed that the teacher wasn't there. I considered that maybe he'd had to take a last-minute bathroom break. Hell, if I had to teach a bunch of sixteen-year-olds, I would need a porta-potty in my classroom for all the nervous diarrhea I'd be brewing.

I looked around the class to see if there was anybody I knew. The only familiar face belonged to a girl I frequently saw in the hallways on my way to gym class. They called her the Human Tampon because one day she got her period while she was wearing all white. It's so sad that one unfortunate moment can create a nickname that lasts forever. Or if you're lucky like me, there's just too much going on for someone to decide on just ONE nickname. Instead they come up with a different one for each moment of complete humiliation. My favorite at that time was "neck pussy," which was given to me by a guy in my class because, and I quote, "Yo neck got more folds than a fat lady's pussy! Imma call you neck pussy!" I truly admire this cultural period. Art is dead.

I looked up toward the door and saw my friend Tara walk into the classroom. Finally someone who didn't refer to me as genitalia hanging from my face.

TARA: Hey, Shane!
ME: Hey!

She stared at me for a little too long.

ME: What?
TARA: I don't see it.
ME: See what?

TARA: The pussy. I mean, I guess I could see how it looks like another mouth on your neck with the flaps and stuff, but not a pussy. A pussy is vertical, not horizontal.

ME: Can we change the subject?

TARA: Can I touch it?

ME: Stop!

TARA: Please! If you let me touch your pussy, I'll let you touch mine.

Interesting offer. But still I had to decline. We both laughed as the bell rang. The teacher still hadn't made an appearance. We all started wondering where he was. Then the Human Tampon piped up.

HUMAN TAMPON: Should we call the office?

RANDOM BOY: Hey, aren't you that girl who shit her pants in the hallway?

HUMAN TAMPON: No. I'm the period girl.

A nerdy-looking girl spoke from the back of the room.

NERDY GIRL: I'm the shit girl.

RANDOM BOY: I thought you were the girl with the neck pussy.

ME: That's me.

RANDOM BOY: Damn. Y'all need name tags.

Just as the conversation was getting self-harm-inducing a man in his forties walked in carrying a surfboard and wearing a Hawaiian shirt unbuttoned down all the way to his belly button. He kind of looked like a teenager who had gotten detention twenty-five years ago and had just been dismissed. From the name on the board, I put together that his name was Mr. Roberts and from the amount of chest hair that was crawling out of his shirt, I assumed his nickname in high school was the Human Sweater.

MR. ROBERTS: Sorry I'm late. The waves were gnarly this morning and there was a food truck selling fish tacos, so you know I had to get one!

He took a bite of a soggy fish taco and a drop of tartar sauce fell from his lip and onto his old-man nipple. Instead of wiping it off with a napkin he rubbed his hand all over it and the chest hair soaked it up. It was the most disgusting thing I'd ever seen in my life but also the most inventive. If *Shark Tank* had been on at the time, he would have been a tough one to beat.

MR. ROBERTS: Alright, let's go around the room and say your name and one thing about yourself that nobody knows. I'll start. My name is Mr. Roberts, and when I was a teenager I hit something with my car, pretty sure it was a person, and I kept going. Probably killed someone. Who's next?

HUMAN TAMPON: My name is Karen—

The students all gasped. She had a name??

KAREN: And I have a pen pal in prison. He's getting out soon. He was in there for murder.

All the students looked at each other, scared. I'm pretty sure her nickname was Don't Fuck with Karen after that.

TARA: My name is Tara and sometimes when I'm sad I watch beheading videos.

MR. ROBERTS: You should probably keep that to yourself. What about you, sir?

He pointed at me. My whole body went numb. The thought of

speaking in front of my class was making me sweat bullets. My neck pussy was very wet and not in a good way.

MR. ROBERTS: Come on. What's your name?
RANDOM BOY: I think it's Neck Pussy, sir.

The class laughed. Mr. Roberts looked at the random boy.

MR. ROBERTS: If that's what you think a vagina looks like, then you must be a virgin as I suspected.

The class laughed even harder. This time AT the random boy. I could feel the tide turning and it gave me the courage to stand up.

ME: My name is Shane. And people don't really know anything about me so I'm having trouble thinking of what to say.
MR. ROBERTS: What do you like to do?
ME: You mean, like, at home?
MR. ROBERTS: Ya, what are your hobbies?

I had to think long and hard about this. I was tempted to tell the class that I liked to go to jackinworld.com and learn new techniques on how to masturbate better but wasn't sure if honesty was the best tactic. It would have just given them even more nickname options. But side note, jackinworld.com is amazing. It taught me how to turn a banana, ziplock bag, and a toilet seat cover into a vagina. Best fake vagina feeling I've ever had. #notanAD #notSPONS

ME: Well . . . I like movies.
MR. ROBERTS: What kind of movies?
ME: I like funny ones. Those are the kind I want to make.

MR. ROBERTS: Oh, so you want to be a director.

ME: Ya, I make some now. But they aren't very good. And the only actor I know is my grandma, so they are all about old people.

MR. ROBERTS: Sounds depressing. I love it! Thank you, Shane.

I sat down with a smile on my face. The students finally knew something about me. Something that didn't end in a punch line. I thought maybe this class was going to change my life. Maybe Mr. Roberts was going to bring me out of my shell. Little did I know he was but not in the way I'd hoped.

The next day when we came into class there was writing on the board that said: "WHAT DO YOU DREAM ABOUT?" I was hoping we wouldn't be going around the room again, because if I told the class my dreams, my new nickname would be Restraining Order. This time, Mr. Roberts strolled into class wearing working gloves and an open flannel shirt.

MR. ROBERTS: Sorry, guys. I was busy building a chair.

What doesn't this guy do? He's a surfer. A wood worker. What's next? I could only pray it was baker.

MR. ROBERTS: We have our first assignment today! It's all about dreams. Partner up with someone and think of a creative way to teach the class about dreams. You can do a song, a dance, or even a short film.

He looked over at me and winked.

MR. ROBERTS: You have a week to do it! We will show all of them next Monday! I can only DREAM of what you are going to come up with. Hopefully it won't be a NIGHTMARE!

We definitely weren't going to add "comedian" to his occupation list.

I partnered up with my friend Tara and we came up with a video concept. We were going to dress up as crazy characters and go around Walmart asking people about their dreams. My character was going to be Leonard Lipshitz and she was going to be Sylvia Brownhole. Character comedy was something I was really passionate about, but I hadn't really told any of my friends that. They knew I was funny because I would joke around with them, but they didn't know I was so into improvisational comedy. When I was a kid I had wanted to grow up and perform on *Saturday Night Live*. They always had a least one fat guy on that show, which gave me hope. It also gave me hope because then I'd be getting paid to be fat, which is WAY better than doing it for free.

Tara and I went to a costume shop to find our characters' looks. I wanted to find something really bizarre, like a sweater made out of Beanie Babies or a tie that was also a rubber chicken. Tara was looking in the "must be over 18" section, and I had to explain to her that showing nipples was probably not going to fly in a high school project.

TARA: Can't you just blur them out? Like on *Cops*?

After we found our costumes it was time to go to Walmart with our camera in hand. Neither of us drove yet, so I asked my mom to join us.

MOM: You want me to be a part of the crew??
ME: Sure!
MOM: What's my call time?!
ME: Um . . . after you finish making us Hot Pockets?
MOM: Got it! You can count on me, Mr. Director!

It was sweet how she was so into it. I'm sure if I'd given her a day's notice she would have embroidered a shirt that said "CREW MEMBER" on it. We got into her car and I turned my camera on. I started interviewing my mom while I was in character. She freaked out.

ME: So, what are your dreams about?

MOM: Wait, are you filming me?

ME: Yup!

MOM: If I'd known, I would have done my makeup! And hair! And gotten a neck lift!

I get my labias from my mother.

ME: So give us a taste of your dreams. Let us into your mind.

MOM: Well, last night I had a dream that you and I moved to a really amazing cabin in Big Bear with a beautiful golden retriever and spent the rest of our lives together! What do you think that means?

ME: I think it means we're WAY too close!

As we pulled up to Walmart I decided it would be funny to park in the handicap spot and force my mom to pretend to have Tourette's. I'm not sure now why that would have warranted a parking spot, but I wasn't really thinking logically at the time. I turned the camera off and gave my mom directions.

ME: Ok, so randomly scream bad words while you are parking the car.

MOM: Oh, Shaney, I can't do that. I don't think God would want me to curse on camera.

ME: It's for the movie. You're the star. Don't you want to make the movie good?

It was the same conversation I'm assuming some directors have with actresses before a nude scene. I guilted her into doing what I wanted. The scary part is if I tried, she probably would have shown the goods.

MOM: Ok. For the movie! Sorry, God!
ME: That's the spirit! And ACTION!

On action my mom started screaming curse words at the top of her lungs. It was amazing to watch. It's how I'd always imagined our conversation in the future going when I came out of the closet. INTENSE. After that we walked into Walmart and started walking up to strangers. This was before YouTube was a thing, so it wasn't normal to see a couple of dumb teenagers with a camera in public. Nowadays you see kids running around the mall taking selfies, vlogging their lives, and pulling pranks on strangers. It's almost like everyone wants to be on camera and make content. Even my mom has a YouTube channel. Granted it's just videos of her dogs swimming in the pool, but it's still "content." Wow. I feel like the word is beginning to become meaningless. I met a YouTuber one time who told me she made content where she would eat all the ingredients of a cake and then vomit them up into a bowl and cook it. She called them Barf Cakes. I love the internet.

After about three hours of walking around Walmart we decided we had enough material to make this video great. I felt super confident about it and couldn't wait to show the class. I was especially excited to show Mr. Roberts and thank him for helping me come out of my shell. It would be the first time my peers saw me in a different light and maybe they would call me the fat funny guy instead of just the fat guy.

Monday arrived pretty quickly, and I was ready! I had taken all week to edit the video, and I felt like I had my masterpiece. It was funny, shocking, and informative. I felt like I was able to make a video that not only had jokes but got all the information across that it needed to. I made sure to hit all the topics that Mr. Roberts wanted us to cover and still get in a few fart jokes. When we got to class the board said, "TODAY'S THE DAY," and I couldn't have been more excited about it.

MR. ROBERTS: Alright, who wants to go first?

For the first time in my life I was going to volunteer for something. I had never put myself out there like this before, but I was so pumped for people to see the video and I couldn't wait to make Mr. Roberts proud.

ME: We will!
MR. ROBERTS: Alright, Shane! What have you prepared?
ME: We made a video. I hope you guys like it.

I walked up to the TV and slipped my videotape into the VCR. My heart was pounding and my fingers were trembling as I pressed the play button. I walked back to my desk and sat down. The static on the TV felt like it lasted forever as all the students waited to see what kind of miracle Neck Pussy had given birth to. Then it started. The first shot was my mom screaming cuss words into the camera. I had bleeped them out because I wanted to keep it appropriate. The entire class erupted in laughter. Some of them were even applauding. A guy sitting behind me started slapping my back.

BACK SLAPPER: That's your momma?! That's shit's so funny, man!!

I was instantly relieved. They got it. They were loving it. As the video continued their laughter only got louder. It was a mixture of Tara and me looking like idiots and us giving actual information. I wanted it to be a parody of a children's educational show on PBS, and I felt like it was really succeeding. I also wanted to make sure it wasn't just dumb for the sake of being dumb; I wanted it still to be smart but full of off-color jokes. The video was just about to reach the climax when the screen went blank. The class yelled in confusion.

BACK SLAPPER: What happened?!
RANDOM BOY: Did the TV break??

The TV was just fine. It was my heart that broke when I looked over at Mr. Roberts, who was holding the remote with a disgusted look on his face. The class got quiet. Everyone looked at him in shock, waiting to see what he was going to say. Tara grabbed my arm and looked at me the same way a cow looks at a butcher before the slaughter.

MR. ROBERTS: Shane. I am very, very shocked and disappointed. What you made was offensive. Disrespectful. Mean-spirited. And above all, not funny in the slightest. I thought you wanted to make movies. Not trash like that. I guess I misjudged you.

To say my heart broke is an understatement. My heart shattered, then got vacuumed up, then was thrown into an incinerator and burned to dust. I didn't understand why he was so upset when the video was obviously getting an amazing reaction from the class. My mind was racing and I didn't know what to say. Not only had a teacher never been mad at me before but I had never shown one of my videos to anyone but my family. This was like falling at the Oscars and the whole world waiting to see how you got up. I gathered as much courage together as I could and I began to speak.

ME: But everyone was laughing.

MR. ROBERTS: See me after class. We can talk about it then.

ME: No. I want to talk about it now. I'm proud of what I made. And everyone in here was loving it. I don't understand why you are so mad at me.

MR. ROBERTS: I said we will talk about it after class.

ME: No! I want to talk about it now.

Mr. Roberts took a deep breath and then asked me to join him outside in the hall. As we walked out of the classroom all the students started mumbling. They were just as confused as I was.

TARA: Good thing I didn't show my nipples.

Mr. Roberts leaned up against a locker and put his hand over his face in aggravation. He seemed so angry and I was so confused. After a few grunts and sighs he finally began to speak.

MR. ROBERTS: Shane. I'm really shocked and disturbed by what you made.

ME: I don't get it. It was funny. And we covered all the material you wanted.

MR. ROBERTS: That was not funny. It was awful and actually made me sick. You don't see what was wrong about it? All the bad language? All the sex jokes?

ME: But nocturnal emissions was something you wanted us to cover.

MR. ROBERTS: Yes, but I didn't want you to do it using sock puppets and hair conditioner.

That scene might have gone a little too far. I admit that. I should have just DESCRIBED wet dreams, not shown it. But a tip to future filmmakers: hair conditioner makes amazing fake semen. Just the right consistency and not as smelly as mayonnaise. You're welcome.

ME: I'm sorry. I just wanted to make something funny. Something like the kinda movies I want to make one day.
MR. ROBERTS: Nobody wants to watch movies like that. Nobody.
ME: But what about the kids in there? They were laughing.
MR. ROBERTS: They were laughing AT it, Shane. There's a difference.

That hit me right in the gut. I knew the difference between getting laughed at and being laughed with. Hell, my whole high school career up until that point consisted of kids calling me names and laughing at me while they did it. But this time was different. They were on my side. I connected with them and knew what they thought was funny. It all hit me, and I started to cry. I didn't know what to say to Mr. Roberts, but I didn't want to say anything I'd regret, so I just walked away.

MR. ROBERTS: Shane, where are you going? Class isn't over yet.
ME: It is for me.

I think the part that hurt the most was that he discounted the entire video because it had a few dirty jokes. He couldn't see past that and consider that I had really worked hard on it and made something I was proud of. Not to mention the fact that the whole class was enjoying it. The whole situation was too much for me to handle emotionally. I walked out of the building and across the campus. I wanted to get as far away from the situation as I could. I went into the gym bathroom and sat down in a stall. I pulled out my flip phone to text my mom. Before I could even type anything I saw that I had a text waiting for me. I opened it up and it was from my mom and it said, "I'm so proud of you. Today other people are going to see what I've seen all along. What a talented, funny, amazing young man you are." I started crying and put my phone back in my backpack. I felt defeated. Until the next day when things turned around.

As I walked into first period Tara came up to me and gave me a hug.

TARA: I'm so sorry. It was a really funny video. I think Mr. Roberts had a bad fish taco or something.

ME: It's ok. I'm just trying to forget it ever happened.

My English teacher walked up behind me and whispered in my ear.

ENGLISH TEACHER: I saw your dreams video. The hardest I've laughed in years. Good job, man. You're sick!

As he walked back to his desk my whole world changed. He got it. A grown man got it. Not just a teenager. Not just my mom. A person who has no reason to lie to me.

TARA: What did he say?

ME: That he liked our video.

TARA: He saw it?? Damn. He's so hot. Maybe I *should* have shown my nipples.

That day every teacher walked up to me throughout the day and told me that they saw the video and loved it. I don't know how they saw it, but I wasn't questioning it. I was just excited my work was getting out there! Later I was called into the principal's office, and I was shocked. I had never been called to the office before, and I was assuming I either did something wrong and I was getting detention or that someone in my family died. Hopefully someone had died. I was terrified of detention.

As I walked into his office the principal asked me to sit in the seat across from him. Principal Williams was a very intense man and always looked like he had just tasted a complicated chili recipe and was trying to figure out the secret ingredient.

PRINCIPAL WILLIAMS: Do you know why you're here, Shane?

ME: Someone died?

PRINCIPAL WILLIAMS: What? No. Who do you think died?

ME: I dunno. Probably someone on my mom's side. They're all obese like me.

PRINCIPAL WILLIAMS: No. No one is dead.

He reached from under his desk and pulled out a videotape. He placed it on his desk and looked up at me.

PRINCIPAL WILLIAMS: Does this look familiar?

ME: Oh. You saw it?

PRINCIPAL WILLIAMS: Oh ya. Mr. Roberts came in here yesterday and showed it to me. He wanted my opinion on how best to deal with the situation.

ME: And?

PRINCIPAL WILLIAMS: And I told him it was hilarious and I had never seen anything like it.

The dust of my heart came back together and formed a big warm clump. I was shocked and overwhelmed. This time in the best way.

PRINCIPAL WILLIAMS: I showed it to all my friends here at work and they thought it was one of the funniest things they'd ever seen. How did you think of all this stuff? You've got quite the imagination there, Shane.

ME: I dunno. I guess it just comes to me.

PRINCIPAL WILLIAMS: Well, keep it up. I can't wait to see the crazy shit you come up with next.

He said "shit." My principal just said "shit." Maybe I was dreaming. If he had said the F word, it would have turned into a full-on wet dream. I love it when teachers cuss.

ME: Did Mr. Roberts tell you what he said to me?

PRINCIPAL WILLIAMS: He did. And I told him I disagreed. Shane, throughout your life some people aren't going to get what you do. Some people are gonna think you're crazy and not give you a fair chance. They won't open up their minds enough to see the potential you have and see all the greatness you have in that head of yours. But there will also be people who do. People that get you. And I'm one of them.

That conversation has stuck with me ever since. It gave me the confidence to keep going and not let what Mr. Roberts said get me down. If anything, what he said lit a fire underneath me to prove him wrong.

PRINCIPAL WILLIAMS: You know I still have to give you detention though, right? You did make a video where you had your mother screaming the C word over and over again.

Damn it. So close.

Looking back, I don't completely fault Mr. Roberts for not liking the video I made. I guess he was looking for more of a "by the books" short film, and mine definitely wasn't. But I'm happy that it happened, because it thickened my skin and got me ready for the criticism that was going to be thrown my way as an adult.

Just like Mr. Roberts, some people still don't get me. They think I'm disgusting. "Human trash" as someone on reddit referred to me once. But there are even more people who understand what I do and appreciate it. For every bad review, there are a hundred like the ones below. And to me, that's all that matters.

"*Not Cool* is an insanely hilarious teen comedy that is a nonstop laugh fest from beginning to end. You will definitely cry at some point . . . but before you can really let loose your tears you will start laughing again. . . . If you enjoy a good laugh out loud comedy that I don't doubt for a minute you WON'T love this movie! I've already seen it 17 times since it came out!"

—Janetlc69

"I bought this movie to support Shane, and honestly expected nobody in my home would be able to keep interest for more than 5 minutes because their humor is very different than mine. BOY, WAS I WRONG! Within 3 minutes, my sister was literally rolling in tears laughing, as was her husband. The jokes were amazing, somewhat controversial, but that's Shane! I wouldn't have imagined his movie any other way . . . Overall, I am giving this movie 10 stars. If I weren't such a fan of Shane's, I honestly think I would still give it 10 stars."

—Zackary

"I'm incredibly proud of you, Shane. You've brought me so much happiness and us fans love you so much and you deserve the world. Thank you."

—Kelly

To everyone who gets me, thank you. To everyone who doesn't, thank you too. You give me the motivation to keep succeeding just to piss you off.

Mom's Chapter:
The Night That
Changed Our Lives
by Teresa Yaw

Note from Shane

My mom has always been a huge inspiration to me, and if you read this whole book, you know what a crucial part of my life she has been. She has always wanted to pursue her dream of being an author, but between working multiple jobs to feed her kids and all the chaos that comes with being a single mother she never had the time. So as a gift to her I decided to hand over the final chapter of this book to her. I told her she could write about whatever she wanted and I wouldn't change a thing. So without further ado, here is a special essay by Teresa Yaw. My mother, my friend, and now a published author. I love you, Mom.

About the Artist

SHANNEN JALAL is an artist from Dublin, Ireland. After having a keen interest in art from a young age, she recently graduated with a degree in visual communications from Dublin Institute of Technology. Her medium of choice is pointillism, a style of illustration in which you create portraits with just dots. You can see her work on her website shannenjalal.com.

I've never been one to call attention to myself because I've always been insecure about my appearance. Not too long ago, the very thought of one of my son's fans running up to me and asking me to take a picture with them would have given me a full-on panic attack. But one night ten years ago something happened that gave me a glimpse into what the future held. What a night that was!

Shane was always a very shy child and stayed to himself a lot. He had a few close friends, but I never really saw him with too many people at one time. I was a single mom who worked a lot of hours and didn't get to spend much time with my kids. Shane stayed very busy with his schoolwork and remained close to home.

One day, he told me to hold a specific night open on my calendar so I could go to his drama production at his high school. I really didn't know what it was about, but I was very excited to go. I requested the early shift so I could get off work in time. I arrived early and decided to sit in the auditorium and just relax. There was a group of kids sitting to my left, and I'm not going to lie, they looked a bit rough to be waiting to watch a drama production. You should never judge a book by its cover, but I still wrote a brief Last Will and Testament on a paper napkin, just in case. Some other kids were busy setting up the stage for the night, and I noticed Shane walking out holding a small desk lamp. Shane had thick, long hair he would hide behind when he walked. I thought, "Well, maybe he is on the

229

set design team." It didn't matter to me because I was so proud of anything he did.

Soon the auditorium started to fill, and I began to wonder where my other sons, Jacob and Jerid, were. They were a handful, and I didn't want to even imagine where they might be. I had saved them seats and prayed they hadn't forgotten. Just as I was about to give up on them, I heard loud laughter, and of course everyone turned around to see where the noise was coming from. Sure enough, it was Jacob and Jerid wrestling with each other down the aisle. "Oh Jesus!" I prayed. "Please don't let them trip and kill some grandma with a cane!" They eventually made it to their seats. My first inclination was to yell at them, but before I could get a word out, a cloud of smoke escaped from Jerid's mouth and hit me in the face, and the smell of weed almost knocked me out. "Jacob, Jerid," I whispered sternly. "How could you do this?" Well, they just laughed even harder, and I was resolved to let it go. As I said, the crowd looked a little rough, so I'm not sure anyone even noticed. On with the show!

The auditorium was now bursting with excited students, parents, and sleeping grandparents. There was feeling of anticipation in the audience that I didn't quite understand, but even I started to feel it moving through my body. Of course, it could have also been the weed vapor hovering over me. Either way, I was enjoying this moment! The curtains parted to reveal the set of a classroom. I recognized a few of Shane's friends and was pretty sure I was correct in thinking Shane was involved in the set design because he was not in the ensemble. As the scene started to play out, I heard whispers from the group of rough kids sitting next to me. "Where is he?" and "I think he comes out soon." I wondered what they were talking about, but I was too scared to ask. Instead I clutched my Last Will and Testament and hoped to God that they weren't planning a shoot-out.

About that time, I heard one of the kids whisper, "There he is!"

I looked up and saw Shane walking out onstage wearing a baggy, hooded sweatshirt and walking with a swagger I had never seen him do before. The group of kids next to me stood up and cheered as if a rock star had just come out onstage! I was so confused about why Shane was up there but even more confused about why so many people were screaming for him. Shane went into character, and with all the confidence of Kanye West snatching Taylor Swift's VMA Award, he swooped down on one of the girls onstage and made his advance. "What is this?" I wondered. How did my shy, little, insecure son become this hysterical, larger-than-life character?

For the next ten minutes I watched the audience laugh, scream, and have so much fun, and it all seemed to center around Shane. Those rough kids sitting to my left were having the best time, and those intimidating looks I had initially observed were now completely lit up. I didn't quite understand what was happening, but I knew it was something big. As I glanced over at Jacob and Jerid, it appeared the weed had worn off, but they too had looks of wonder on their faces. Shane was the brother who stayed to himself, certainly didn't show any resemblance to the cool guys on *SNL*, and in just that quick moment in time was inspiring awe and amazement in his older siblings.

There was a brief intermission, which allowed me a moment to absorb what had just taken place. My mind wandered back to those Saturday nights Shane and I would spend together. He wasn't yet at the age when he would spend time on the weekends with his friends. We looked forward to those simple but special times together. The first thing we would do was drop Jerid off at Knott's Berry Farm so he could hang out with his friends. That was the cool thing back then. Maybe it still is; some things are timeless. After dropping him off we would go buy whatever the latest CD was. We started with *NOW That's What I Call Music!* Volume 1, if you can believe that.

They must be on volume 3,001 at this point. We would drive for hours listening, laughing, and dreaming of what the future might hold for us.

With a *plunk*, I was suddenly brought back to reality as Jerid plopped himself down in his seat with half a churro sticking out of his mouth. The show continued. After a couple of short skits that Shane wasn't in, the curtain opened to a family living room scene, and again the audience began to call out Shane's name. I couldn't wait to see what was going to happen next. It was a hysterical skit about a family from Minnesota, and Shane played the father. I hadn't laughed so hard in years, and I definitely could have used some bladder protection.

Watching my son shine onstage, I could feel the many hardships from the previous nine years melt away. Each day had its share of worries, and it had started to catch up with me. That evening I laughed so hard and was so surprised, I felt new life flow through my body. As the show came to an end and all the students came forward to bow, again I had the joy of hearing the auditorium rumble with the shouts of "Shane! Shane!" That shy little guy, who I worried every day for, stood proudly onstage, and his face lit up any darkness that tried to squeeze in. Jacob and Jerid were shouting, "You're the man, Shane! You're the Man!!" It was as if the earth had turned a new direction and I got to be a part of it.

The excitement continued as I watched the students step down from the stage and all the kids in the audience run toward Shane. For just a second, I considered throwing myself in front of the "rough" kids, but by then I realized they were as wonderful and special as every student in that building.

I slowly made my way out to the lobby as Shane's friends ran up to me and gave lots of hugs. For Jacob, Jerid, and myself, we had just had the most amazing night. There were no worries, there were no fears, there was no sadness, just a joy that seemed to embrace us as a family. After several minutes, I finally got to hug Shane and get through the crowd. With tears in my eyes, I told him it had been the best night of my life. As he looked at me I could almost hear his mind thinking, "It is only the beginning, Mom." I decided to let him enjoy the rest of the evening and head out to my car. As I made my way down the auditorium steps, I turned back around. Time seemed to stand still for just a moment and I heard God's soft voice in my ear say, "Tonight you witnessed an auditorium full of love for Shane. One day, Teresa, you will witness the world loving him." I got to my car and wept. Not tears of pain, but tears of joy and hope.

Nearly ten years have passed since that night at Lakewood High School, and every time I see a crowd gather around Shane and express such love, I think of that special evening that would forever change our lives. I've met so many of Shane's fans since he started on YouTube, and every one of them is more full of love than the last.

Granted the first time I was recognized in public was not such a lovely experience. One day I was walking around the mall and was stopped by an angry-looking woman. She pointed at the shirt I was wearing, which happened to have Shane's face on it, and she said, "I know who you are, and I think your son is disgraceful!!" I stood there in shock for a moment. Then after a few seconds I started laughing and quickly texted Shane. "I got recognized, son!! I'm so excited!!" I still have my Shane Dawson T-shirt, and every time I wear it I think about that lady and get the biggest smile on my face. One person's "disgraceful" is another person's "HERO."

Acknowledgments

This book wouldn't have been possible without the help of so many amazing people. It also wouldn't have been possible without the help of so many food-delivery employees who kept me emotionally eating while writing it. I spent approximately $2,540 on takeout during the creation of this book. Fuck my life.

But the other people who helped inspire and motivate me are priceless. Except for my agents and lawyer. They cost about 15 percent. Still not as much as my food bill though. Instead of just listing all the people who I want to thank, I decided it would be more fun if I gave their name, their role in the process, and what celebrity they remind me of. So here we go. Let's hope I don't end up offending everyone I'm thankful for. I already do enough of that at Thanksgiving when I let everyone know that "I'm most thankful I live an hour away from most of my family members." Ya, doesn't always get the laugh I'm going for.

Sarah Branham	My Editor	Nicole Kidman if she was younger and could move her face.
Judith Curr	My Publisher	Rachael Zoe if she had a healthy BMI and an accent. Judith has a great wardrobe.
Carolyn Reidy	President & CEO of Simon & Schuster	Hillary Clinton. She's so powerful. So smart. I want to be her.
Haley Weaver	Editorial Assistant	Lindsay Lohan if she made better choices.
Ariele Fredman	My Publicist	That dog from *Air Bud*. Not the looks, just the essence. Hopeful. Loyal. A LOT of energy.
Jackie Jou	My Marketing Manager	Simba from *The Lion King*. Once again, not the looks. Just the essence. Feisty. Sweet. Spontaneous dancing.
Brent Weinstein	My Agent	A guy from the Food Network, but I don't remember his name at the moment. I think it's a show where he cooks for people in prison.
Natalie Novak	My Agent	Not that girl from *The Hills* who was super-fucking-annoying. Her friend.
Ali Barash	My Agent	I'm gonna be honest. It's a porn star. But not a fake-looking one, a "homemade" one. Trust me, it's a compliment.
Matthew Saver	My Lawyer	Richard Gere without all the butt rumors. If you don't know what I'm talking about, Google it. You'll fall into a dark hole. Pun intended.

Chris Worthington	My Assistant	A grown-up version of Daniel Radcliffe. I know he's technically a grown-up, but he still looks twelve. Maybe he has a disorder. In that case, I apologize for my insensitivity.
Jerid Yaw	My Brother	The guy from *MythBusters*. Spot-on. It's actually uncanny.
Teresa Yaw	My Mother	Like Julianne Moore if she smiled more. I'm not sure what's wrong with her. I hope she's ok.
Chad Morgan	My First Boyfriend	Chris Pratt but when he was still a human and not a sex robot. Seriously, who made him? Apple? Can someone terminate him so other guys can have a chance?
Lisa Schwartz	My First Girlfriend	The perfect blend of Hilary Duff and the pig from *Babe*. Not the pig's body, just its personality.